FIRST EDITION

PRIMER ON LEARNING AND CONDITIONING

A QUANTITATIVE APPROACH

By Federico Sanabria

Arizona State University

cognella® ACADEMIC PUBLISHING

Bassim Hamadeh, CEO and Publisher
Gem Rabanera, Project Editor
Christian Berk, Associate Production Editor
Jess Estrella, Senior Graphic Designer
Trey Soto, Licensing Associate
Joyce Lue, Interior Designer
Natalie Piccotti, Senior Marketing Manager
Kassie Graves, Vice President of Editorial
Jamie Giganti, Director of Academic Publishing

Cover image copyright © 2017 iStockphoto LP/Pavel_R.

Printed in the United States of America.

ISBN: 978-1-63189-421-3 (pbk) / 978-1-63189-420-6 (br)

To Beatriz

CONTENTS

PREFACE   VII

INTRODUCTION   IX

CHAPTER 1: INTRODUCTION   **1**

Purpose and Scope   1

Historical Background   8

Animal Subjects in Behavioral Research   12

References   13

CHAPTER 2: KEY CONCEPTS   **17**

Fundamental Terms   17

The Design of a Conditioning Experiment   19

Variables   19

Designing a Conditioning Experiment   21

Conditioning Experiments Focused on Learning   22

Conditioning Experiments Focused on Performance   23

Functional Relations and their Graphical Representation   24

Types of Functions   25

References   29

CHAPTER 3: UNCONDITIONED BEHAVIOR   **31**

Reflexes and Modal Action Patterns   31

Repeated Presentations of an Unconditioned Stimulus   35

Investigating Non-Associative Learning   39

Exercises   42

References   43

CHAPTER 4: PAVLOVIAN CONDITIONING   **45**

Demonstrating Pavlovian Conditioning   47

The Temporal Arrangement of CS and US   50

Experimental Paradigms   51

Learning Mechanisms   53

    The Rescorla-Wagner model   54

Exercises   59

References   61

CHAPTER 5: FUNDAMENTALS OF OPERANT CONDITIONING   **63**

Basic Concepts   64

Simple Schedules of Reinforcement   72

Exercises   79

References   80

CHAPTER 6: ADVANCED CONCEPTS IN OPERANT CONDITIONING   **83**

Compound Schedules of Reinforcement   83

Choice Behavior   86

Intertemporal Choice and Self-Control   92

Behavioral Economics   95

Mechanisms of Reinforcement   98

Exercises   99

References   100

PREFACE

My first learning and conditioning course as an undergraduate student had a component that is becoming unusual: a laboratory section. The manual for that section was C. S. Reynold's (1968) *A Primer on Operant Conditioning*. By that time, Reynold's text was already outdated, but it was a useful introduction to the practical aspects of research on learning. Since then, dozens of textbooks on learning have been published, but very few are infused with the pragmatic approach of Reynold's 50-year-old book.

The book you are now holding, however, is not meant to be a laboratory manual. Instead, it focuses on another practical aspect of behavior analysis that is often overlooked, when not explicitly avoided: quantification. Over the last few decades, as applied behavior analysis has impacted areas as disparate as special education, organizational behavior, and substance abuse, basic behavior analysis has embraced mathematical models with growing enthusiasm, giving rise to organizations such as the Society for the Quantitative Analysis of Behavior. Mathematization is at the center of modern natural sciences, and evidence for its utility in basic learning research is only increasing. Many of the artificial intelligence systems that are becoming prevalent in science, technology, and in our daily lives are, at the most basic level, learning algorithms inspired by the mathematical regularities of natural behavior.

As an introductory text, this book does not pretend to expose the reader to all the topics that the field of learning comprises. Extinction learning, generalization, and stimulus control are addressed as part of broader topics. Punishment and aversive control are only briefly discussed. It is my hope that the concepts discussed in the book lay the foundation for the deeper treatment that these topics require. Nonetheless, subjects that are more amenable to quantitative analysis, such as behavioral economics and the Rescorla-Wagner model of associative learning, are examined in particular detail.

It is somewhat ironic that most textbooks on learning fail to adopt a key learning principle: that learning happens by doing, not just by listening or reading. Active learning is a redundancy—there is no such thing as passive learning. In that spirit, I mean for this book to be a concise and practical complement to classroom lectures and activities, not a substitute for them. It contains exercises that may be solved individually or in groups and that are primarily intended to initiate discussions. The book aims at making somewhat complex ideas intuitive, but not at the cost of protracted examples. Key concepts are highlighted, but their importance is not extensively justified. Applications beyond the scope of basic learning are kept to a minimum.

In its concise volume, Reynold afforded his readers the language necessary to understand the scientific literature on learning in his time period. Times have changed, and we need to update our language. I can only hope that his book serves that mission, even if imperfectly.

INTRODUCTION

The organization of this book mostly follows the traditional layout of learning textbooks. The text, however, is interleaved with questions the reader should answer in order to move on. These questions are fairly open ended and can be used as assignments for further discussion in the classroom. Readers are encouraged to stop and ask for help before proceeding if they find themselves stuck on one of these questions.

The end of some chapters include exercises, some of which are more challenging and require particular answers. These exercises are meant to assess mastery of the material covered in each chapter. I encourage students to complete these exercises individually and to compare their solutions to those of other students. Exams may be built from variations of these exercises.

All the material included in the book assumes no mathematical background beyond high school algebra. Although all exercises may be solved by hand, students are encouraged to use a spreadsheet software package such as Microsoft Excel® to visualize concepts, particularly when solving some of the exercises.

To preclude ambiguity in the use of key terms, the book makes heavy use of nomenclature and acronyms that are fairly standard in the field. Learning this jargon early on facilitates an intuitive understanding, which makes use of the material easier, both while reading the book and while holding discussions in the classroom.

Chapter 1 includes a brief conceptual and historical perspective on the ideas that will be discussed in the rest of the book. Of particular importance is the concept of learning, which defines the scope of this book. Chapter 2 delves deeper into some key conceptual issues, such as the distinction between environment and organism, and stimulus and response. It also provides the elements for designing conditioning experiments and representing functional relations, which are the foundation of many exercises.

Chapter 3 covers simple environment-response relations that are foundational to more complex forms of learning. Concepts such as modal action pattern, generalization gradient, habituation, and sensitization are introduced in this chapter. Chapter 4 discusses elementary forms of associative learning. It couches key associative-learning phenomena, such as excitatory and inhibitory conditioning, overshadowing, blocking, latent inhibition, and post-extinction effects in the context of the Rescola-Wagner model.

Chapter 5 distinguishes operant conditioning from Pavlovian conditioning, elaborating on key concepts such as operant contingency, reinforcement and punishment, and simple schedules of reinforcement. Chapter 6 builds on these concepts to introduce more complex schedules of reinforcement, with a focus on concurrent schedules and their role in the assessment of choice and preference. These topics are further elaborated to discuss self-control and behavioral economics and their implications for the mechanisms of reinforcement.

BACKGROUND

PURPOSE AND SCOPE

This book is intended to provide an introduction to fundamental concepts in learning and conditioning from a quantitative perspective. To clarify this objective, three concepts must be defined first: *learning*, *conditioning*, and *quantitative perspective*.

Learning. This is a concept we use very often in various situations. We say that "Annie is a fast learner" and that "Ben has a hard time learning how to play the flute." When someone does something stupid repeatedly, we often say, "He never learns!" Like so many other concepts, however, the fact that we often use the word "learning" does not mean that we understand, with precision, what we mean by it. We can get by with this ambiguity in a normal conversation (imagine if we had to define every word we said!), but a science of learning requires a more clear definition of that term.

A simple method to understand a common concept is to examine in detail how it is normally used. In the box, provide three real situations in which someone learns something (e.g., "Annie learned how to bake an apple pie"). For each example, identify who learned what.

Box 1.1

Notice that in each example you identified an *individual* who learns *something*. This leads us to the first component of a definition of learning: *It is something that an individual organism acquires.* This preliminary definition applies, of course, to non-human animals: dogs learn new tricks; bees learn about the location of certain flowers. It may also apply to non-living things, particularly computers, that acquire certain abilities. Think, for instance, of your Netflix account learning your movie preferences, or a robot learning your name. Nonetheless, it is useful to distinguish between the *natural learning* of living organisms, and the *artificial learning* (or *artificial intelligence*) of machines and computers. Natural learning is something that we do not fully understand and that we can investigate scientifically; artificial learning is something that is engineered into objects for pre-specified purposes. What we discover about natural learning may inform the design of learning machines (Sutton & Barto, 1998), and artificial-learning algorithms often inspire hypotheses about natural learning (Schultz, 1998). To be clear, though, the focus of this book is the natural learning of individual living organisms, to which we will refer to simply as *learning*.

Our definition of *individual organism* is very broad, it includes the obvious: you, your cat, even fruit flies and worms. Can you think of someone or something that doesn't fall into this definition but should? (e.g., is the chair you are sitting in an individual organism that can learn?) Think hard; if you come up with an example, write it in the box; otherwise, write "Nope, nothing."

Box 1.2

Our preliminary definition sets some limits to who or what can learn, at least in the sense in which we use this verb here. For instance, sometimes it is said that "institutions learn" (e.g., "the Department of Treasury learned about the money laundering practices of a corrupt company"). Institutions, however, are not individuals in the sense of our preliminary definition. Institutions are organizations and practices that, by definition, comprise multiple individuals. Thus, for the purposes of this book, we will not be concerned with how institutions, organizations, and groups learn. (This, of course, does not exclude individuals learning *in the context of* an institution, or learning *about* an institution).

Read our preliminary definition of learning again: *It is something that an individual organism acquires.* What is that *something*? It may be a skill, information, maybe even a preference. It is certainly not an object—it is not something that we can grab, touch, point at, etc. It is something more abstract. To define an abstract term, it is probably a good idea to identify the conditions in which we normally use that term. For instance, how do you know that someone has acquired a particular skill, knows something, or has developed a particular preference? Let's try a specific situation. How would you determine whether your (hypothetical) cousin Ben has the ability to ride a bicycle without training wheels?

Box 1.3
_____

In your example, it is very likely that you included some form of a *test* of Ben's bicycling dexterity under specific conditions. This means that anything that may be learned has to be testable. Furthermore, appropriate testing enhances our certainty that someone has learned something. Even if we casually see Ben riding a bicycle without training wheels, it is possible that he is using some stabilizing technology that we ignore; to be sure, we should test his ability in a bicycle that we have examined.

Learning, we have agreed so far, is the acquisition of a testable skill, knowledge, or preference by an individual organism. Now, what do we mean by *acquisition*? We generally mean that the individual organism was not born with the skill, knowledge, or preference that we say was learned. The ability to close my eyes when dirt is blown into them is not something that is acquired; most animals with eyes and eyelids are born with this ability. This implies that learning something involves a change in test performance that is caused by some experience.

But, does any experience count as a potential cause of learning? Consider the case of Mr. Z, who developed extraordinary mechanical abilities at age nine immediately after a bullet wounded his brain (Brink, 1980). Would you say that Mr. Z learned these abilities because of his head-wound experience? Probably not. Learning involves not just any experience, but the experience of the relation between changes in behavior (i.e., in what the organism does) and/or changes in stimuli (i.e., in the environment). The *and/or* conjunction means that a learning experience may comprise behavior-stimulus relations (e.g., Ben learning that pedaling results in forward motion) and stimulus-stimulus relations (e.g., Carol learning that a particular shade of brown indicates that the pie crust is ready). It is important to keep in mind that the behavior of one organism may serve as stimulus to another organism.

It is very easy to mistakenly infer learning from changes in test performance that do not involve learning. Suppose that you tested Ben's bicycle riding skills a week ago and he performed in such way that you judged he did not possess the ability to ride a bicycle without training wheels. Now, you test Ben again and he demonstrates impressive skills. Does this mean that Ben learned to ride a bicycle during the last week? Can you think of what (other than learning) may account for Ben's improvement in performance?

Box 1.4

Here are two other examples: (1) Ben had hurt one of his feet last week, but it healed this week; (2) Ben rode his bicycle a lot just prior to your test last week and wanted to do something else, but today he was excited about riding his bicycle. In both examples Ben might have had the ability to ride a bicycle a week ago, but in the first example he *could not* ride a bicycle because of a sensorimotor impediment, and in the second example he *did not want to* ride a bicycle. That is, learning may be confounded with changes in *sensorimotor capacity* (example 1) and with changes in *motivation* (example 2). To which of these categories does your example in 1.4 belong? Or does it belong to a different category not considered?

Box 1.5

There are many other reasons, aside from these examples, for why test performance may change over time even when learning is not involved. Fatigue (Ben was tired; now he is not), maturation (Ben could not reach the pedals; now he does), and pharmacological effects (Ben was drowsy due to some cough medicine) are just a few of those reasons. All these alternative explanations, however, fall into one of the two categories already mentioned: sensorimotor and motivational changes. Learning experiences may involve sensorimotor and motivational changes, but they do not involve *just* those changes. Most important right now, however, is the distinction between *learning* and *performance*. Appropriate performance in a test requires the right sensorimotor, motivational, and training conditions— missing any of these may hurt performance in a test, even if the target skill or knowledge was learned (Figure 1.1).

Given all these considerations, we are ready to form a definition of learning. Learning is *the acquisition by an individual organism, through experience, of the disposition to perform, given the appropriate testing conditions, a specific behavior.* By *disposition* we mean the increased probability of behaving in a particular way. We say that Ben learns to ride his bicycle when he acquires a disposition to perform a bicycle-riding behavior if asked to ride a bicycle. Even if he is never tested for this ability, the fact that Ben *can* perform well in an appropriate test and that such ability was acquired through experience suffices to say that Ben learned to ride a bicycle.

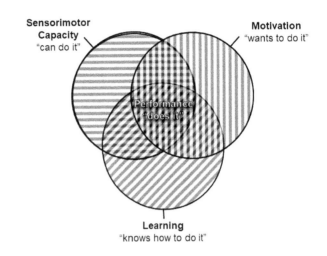

Figure 1.1. Performance in a learning test requires not only learning the target ability, but also the sensorimotor capacity and motivation to perform.

The proposed definition of *learning* is broad, because the term *disposition* encompasses a wide range of behavioral phenomena. It involves not only the probability of doing something (e.g., playing a musical instrument), but also the probability of *not* doing something (e.g., not putting your hand on a hot stove). It may involve emotional responses such as disgust and fear. It is likely that being disgusted at the idea of eating a pet or being afraid of crowds are learned dispositions (Lissek et al., 2005; Yeomans, 2006). Moreover, the proposed definition of learning does not distinguish between procedural and declarative learning. The former refers to the acquisition of abilities and skills such as riding a bicycle or playing video games. The latter refers to the acquisition of knowledge about things, such as that the Earth orbits the Sun, or that Paris is the capital of France. The procedural-declarative distinction is a useful one, in part because each type of learning appears to depend on a separate neural substrate (Ashby & O'Brien, 2005). This distinction, however, is beyond the scope of this primer.

Given the definitions provided here, think of a situation that involves learning but that most people would not recognize as involving learning (or vice versa). Why do you think this mismatch between our definition and the normal use of the term *learning* happens?

Box 1.6

Conditioning. In the sense in which it is used here, *conditioning* is a more technical term than *learning*; it is rarely used in a normal conversation (and, when it is, it is often used incorrectly). Therefore, we will not seek to match this term with its colloquial use, but instead start out with a definition that matches its technical use over decades of learning research. *Conditioning is an experimental training procedure in which an organism is exposed to a particular arrangement of stimuli, and that arrangement causes a particular response to some of those stimuli.*

Let's apply this definition to a specific training situation, that of conditioned salivation in dogs. In his paradigmatic experiment, Pavlov (1927)—of whom we will have more to say later in this chapter—presented dogs with the sound of a metronome right before giving them meat powder (Figure 1.2). This is the *experimental training procedure* in the definition of conditioning. The dog is the target organism, the sound and meat powder are the stimuli, and they are arranged in a particular way: the sound immediately precedes the food. This arrangement causes a particular response to one of the stimuli—it makes the dogs salivate in response to the sound.

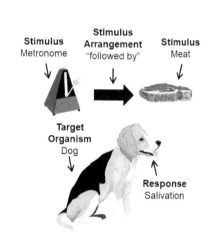

Figure 1.2. Illustrative conditioning experiment. An organism (dog) is exposed to a particular arrangement of stimuli (sound of a metronome followed by meat powder), and that arrangement causes a particular response (salivation) to some of those stimuli (sound of metronome).

Following the definition of learning in the previous section, it may be said that, through conditioning, the dog in Figure 1.2 learned to salivate to the sound of the metronome: it acquired, through experience, a disposition to salivate when tested with a sound. Conditioning always results in learning. It is important, however, to keep in mind that the dog learned to salivate to the sound *because of* the temporal relation between sound and food during training. "Salivation to the sound" only describes the performance of the dog during the test. Because of the training that caused such performance, we know that the dog learned not simply to salivate to the sound—it learned that the sound precedes food.

Conditioning implies a causal relation between training procedure and test performance. Causation can only be demonstrated through experimentation. That is, for an investigator to claim that A caused B, he or she should control A in such way that demonstrates that when A is present, so is B, and when A is absent, B is absent too. This is how we normally demonstrate, for instance, that a particular switch causes a light in the room to turn on: We control the switch in such way that we can demonstrate that when the switch is on, so is the light, and when it is off, the light is off too. To demonstrate that Pavlov's dogs salivate to the sound because of the temporal relation between sound and food during training, an experiment is needed to show that when such temporal relation is present, the dogs salivate to the sound, and when it is absent, the dogs salivate significantly less to the sound. The former training arrangement (with the temporal relation present) is known as the *experimental condition*; the latter (with the temporal relation absent) is known as the *control condition*. To demonstrate conditioning, experimentation is required, which means implementing the appropriate control condition.

It is a common mistake to use the terms *learning* and *conditioning* as if they have the same meaning. For instance, when I see lightning, I may cover my ears to avoid the loud thunder that typically follows. If someone were to try to explain my behavior, she may say, "It is conditioned," by which she means

"It is due to the consistent experience that lightning is followed by thunder." The latter hypothesis is plausible, but the claim that it is conditioned is a misuse of the term. No experimenter controlled the presence and absence of lightning and thunder, and there was no control condition. Indeed, as in the case of the salivating dog, conditioning results in learning, but conditioning is not learning. Look at the definition again: *Conditioning is an experimental procedure*; learning is what results from that procedure.

Apply the definition of conditioning to your own example. Identify the organism, the stimuli, how these stimuli are arranged, and what response to what stimulus should occur after training.

Box 1.7

Organism:

Stimuli:

Arrangement:

Response:

A quantitative perspective. Because of its precision, mathematics has become, over the course of the last few centuries, the *lingua franca* of science. The science of learning is not an exception to this development. Fortunately, appreciating the most successful quantitative models of learning and conditioning at an introductory level does not require a level of mathematics beyond high school algebra—the level of mathematics assumed for this book.

A science of learning aims at identifying the factors that facilitate or interfere with the acquisition of new behaviors. These factors are evaluated against performance in conditioning tests. We may ask, for instance, whether presenting conditioning trials (sound-food pairings in the salivating dog example) in rapid succession results in more effective conditioning than spacing them. Ultimately, we may draw mathematical functions that relate learning factors against performance. These functions are important, because (a) their parameters (e.g., the slope and intercept of a straight line) may constitute key components of the mechanism by which organisms learn, and (b) they are empirically testable. In short, couching our intuitions and hypotheses about learning in mathematical terms may aid in advancing our understanding of how learning happens.

Just like it is difficult to learn how to ride a bicycle by reading about it, it is difficult to learn about mathematical models of learning, even at an introductory level, by simply reading about them. This book includes exercises that involve manipulating the variables of the most successful models in the field and tracking the predicted effects of these manipulations. Through these exercises, you should become familiar with the intuition behind each model.

HISTORICAL BACKGROUND

Modern learning research is rooted mainly in two scholarly traditions. The first tradition is the philosophical investigation of associative learning. The second tradition is the biological study of behavior. Together, these traditions provide a historical context to current research in learning.

The early associationist tradition. The philosophical tradition in learning was (and to some extent still is) concerned with how ideas are formed. When we think of something concrete (e.g., an apple) or abstract (e.g., happiness), a particular idea comes to mind. Where does that idea come from? Some philosophers argued that some of these ideas must be formed prior to experience, because they make experience possible. Immanuel Kant, for instance, argued that without the ideas of time, space, and causality, we would not be able to build new ideas from experience. Other philosophers, such as David Hartley and David Hume, were more concerned with the particular processes by which we acquire new ideas from experience. Their main argument was that experiences and ideas are associated through rather specific rules to form new ideas, and this ultimately forms the basis of our knowledge. For instance, while interacting with apples, we may hear the word "apple," see multiple apples of various shapes and colors, taste various apples, etc. Because all these experiences often happen together, we come to associate them into a single idea of "apple," which is evoked when someone says "apple" or when we see one (Figure 1.3).

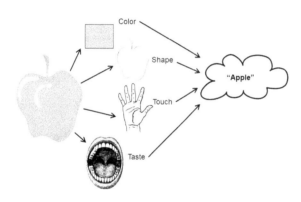

Figure 1.3. The classic associationist explanation for how we learn what is an apple: When experiencing an apple, various features are present simultaneously—its color, shape, taste, etc. Because of their simultaneity, these features are associated into a single idea of "apple."

A critical transition in this philosophical tradition of learning research took place when Wilhelm Wundt began testing the associationist argument experimentally. To do this, Wundt set up what is now considered the first laboratory of psychology at the University of Leipzig in 1879. In his experiments, participants were trained to bring ideas to conscious attention and to decompose them into elementary sensations and ideas. A participant might have been asked to think about an apple and to isolate its color, texture, tactile properties, and memories associated with the idea of "apple." This research method is known as *introspection* and its purpose is to unveil the "chemistry" of ideas: how they are associated, how such associations may be broken up, or how they may form even more complex associations, etc. (Much like computer science and network theory today, chemistry was at the cutting edge of science in the mid-late 19th century and, also much like today, psychology borrowed from the latest trends in science to formulate its own models.)

In the early 20th century, many psychologists raised serious methodological concerns regarding the use of introspection to study consciousness. In particular, psychologists were aware that introspection-based research did not yield observable measures on which multiple investigators could agree. You and I can agree on what "boiling water" is, so that we can independently verify that, when its temperature is raised to 100° C,

Figure 1.4. Wilhelm Wundt (1832–1920) tested the associationist hypothesis of learning in his laboratory using the method of introspection.

water boils. No such agreement was possible with introspection because the key "measures" were hidden inside the introspecting participant. This crisis in experimental psychology promoted the "behaviorist revolt," led by John B. Watson at Johns Hopkins University. Watson argued forcefully not only against the method of introspection, but also against consciousness as an object of study in psychology (this was likely aided by psychoanalytic theories promulgating that consciousness was far less important in the psychic lives of humans than was then thought). Watson argued that psychology should focus on behavior, that is, on what living organisms actually do (Watson, 1913) and hailed the research of a Russian physiologist named Ivan Pavlov as a model for the future of psychology.

Figure 1.5. John B. Watson (1878–1958) proposed a behavioristic approach to psychology, based on the study of what living organisms do.

The Darwinian influence. Early in the history of physiology, there was substantial evidence that movement and behavior depend on the nervous system and that the brain plays an important role in controlling behavior. It was clear, also, that our biological makeup, including our nervous system, was not drastically different from that of other animals. During the 17th, 18th, and a large portion of the 19th century, the notion that the brain controls behavior co-existed in relative harmony with the idea that experiences are turned into ideas in a non-material plane called the *mind*. The notion of parallel biological and mental processes controlling behavior and mind is often referred to as *psychological dualism*, or *mentalism*. So, what happened in the middle of the 19th century that discredited this notion in scientific psychology? Darwin happened.

Darwin is best known for promulgating the theory of evolution of species through natural selection (Darwin, 1859). The idea is simple, yet very powerful: Species have a combination of traits that support the procurement of resources (e.g., food, mates) necessary for reproduction. These traits vary across individuals, and thus resource procurement and reproductive success also vary across individuals. Those individuals with higher reproductive success promote their traits in the niche they occupy. As a result of this process, the prevalent traits of a species are highly adapted to the demands of the niche for resource procurement. For instance, Darwin noticed that the beak of finches varies among the islands that compose the Galápagos archipelago. In islands where fruit and nuts were

Figure 1.6. Charles R. Darwin (1809–1882) promulgated the theory of evolution of species through natural selection. He investigated the expression of emotions in primates as adaptive traits.

prevalent, so were finches with large claw-shaped beaks that could break these foods; in islands where insects were prevalent, so were finches with thin, sharp beaks that could capture these insects more effectively.

The impact of Darwin's findings in biology was enormous, and the (then nascent) science of psychology was not immune to his ideas. Darwin emphasized two ideas of particular importance to psychology: (1) Key traits of a species are an adaptation to significant challenges in the environment where the species evolved[1]; our eyes, for instance, efficiently capture light from the environment, permitting navigation; and (2) Common ancestry of different species is often revealed in the shared features of those species.[2] For instance, most mammals share key features of their reproductive, circulatory, auditory, and central

1 This is not true for *all* traits, but for many of them (Gould & Lewontin, 1979).

2 This similarity is called *homology*. It is also possible for species to develop similar features from different ancestors, because their changes converge on a similar solution to a shared challenge from the environment (e.g., wings in bats and in birds). This kind of similarity is called *homoplasy*.

nervous systems. Nineteenth-century psychologists wondered whether these ideas of adaptation and common ancestry might apply to mental faculties such as reasoning and consciousness, then the focus of psychology. Darwin himself considered these possibilities, providing substantial evidence that the expression of emotions is an adaptive trait shared among primates, including humans (Darwin, 1872). It soon became evident that many mental faculties previously ascribed to humans alone were, at least in part, shared with other species. The field of *comparative psychology* was thus born, introducing the notion that psychological processes, such as learning, could be studied in non-human species (Morgan, 1891; Thorndike, 1911). It is in this context that the study of consciousness, through introspection, fell in disfavor, and principles closely related to comparative psychology, such as a focus on the careful examination of behavior, gained traction in mainstream psychology.

Ivan Pavlov. By the early 20th century, the associative-learning and biological-psychology traditions were bound for convergence. Although Wundt's experimental program had hit a dead end in the introspection method, there was no reason to believe that the hypotheses regarding the mental mechanisms involved in learning were not testable. Comparative psychologists, on the other hand, had developed research methods that were consistent with broader scientific principles (objectivity, reproducibility, etc.) and were on the lookout for psychological processes on which their methods could be applied. Convergence between these two traditions happened almost by accident in Ivan Pavlov's laboratory at the Institute of Experimental Medicine in St. Petersburg, Russia. Pavlov was a physiologist interested in how digestive glands work—he received a Nobel Prize in 1904 for his work. He called the response of these glands to food stimuli *digestive*

Figure 1.7. Ivan P. Pavlov (1849–1936) was awarded the 1904 Nobel Prize for Physiology or Medicine for his work on digestion. He initiated the study of conditioned reflexes.

reflexes. Using dogs as experimental subjects, Pavlov noticed that some of these glands, most noticeably the salivary glands, became active not just when food was placed in the dog's mouth, but also when dogs *saw* the food and, more perplexing, when dogs saw just the person that fed them. Most researchers would have treated these responses as a nuisance, because they indicated a breach in strict experimental control. Not Pavlov. He became interested in how sensory modalities such as vision and hearing could control feeding behavior. He called the physiological responses to arbitrary visual and auditory stimuli *conditioned reflexes* (Pavlov, 1927).

Conditioned reflexes occur when stimuli are correlated in the environment. One such correlation, for instance, is the sight of food with the ingestion of food. When the sight of food regularly precedes the ingestion of food, the mere sight of food may elicit pre-ingestion responses, including salivation. Pavlov studied various factors that influence conditioned reflexes. Over time, it became evident that his research was delving into the much broader question of how stimuli are associated in the mind. Pavlov developed the methodology, borrowed from physiology, to study this question scientifically.

Burrhus F. Skinner and radical behaviorism. Pavlov's research soon inspired a large amount of psychological research, particularly in the United States. This approach to psychology was known as *behaviorism*. In a seminal paper, Burrhus F. Skinner, a behaviorist at Harvard University, identified two types of conditioned reflexes (Skinner, 1935). Mainly, Pavlov's conditioned reflexes (which Skinner called "Type II") are elicited by one stimulus because of its correlation with another stimulus. A conditioned reflex may also occur because a stimulus signals the availability of a second stimulus, whose presentation (or removal) is dependent on the reflex. Skinner argued that this second reflex (which he called "Type I") is significantly different from the first one. Eventually, Skinner would call the process by which Type I conditioned reflexes are formed *operant* or *instrumental conditioning* (Skinner, 1938); those by which Type II reflexes are formed would be known as *classical* or *Pavlovian conditioning*. Skinner would argue that most behavior, particularly in humans, is the product of operant processes (Skinner, 1953). Skinner went further and promulgated the idea that conditioned behavior is not just a vehicle to investigate mental associations, but that it is, on its own, the subject matter of a legitimate branch of science (Skinner, 1950). Skinner's brand of behaviorism, known as *radical behaviorism* (Day, 1983), is very pragmatic: It is particularly concerned with how behavior can be influenced, and thus had (and still has) a major impact in a wide range of fields, from special education to organizational behavior.

Figure 1.8. Burrhus F. Skinner (1904–1990) pioneered the research on operant conditioning and promulgated radical behaviorism.

Modern learning research. So, what does learning research look like now, in the first half of the 21st century? It is very diverse. The Pavlovian and radical traditions of behaviorism are very much alive and expanding, and new approaches to learning have emerged, some merging aspects of both approaches (e.g., Talmi, Seymour, Dayan, & Dolan, 2008), some developing entirely new conceptual frameworks (e.g., Hursh, 1984). Pavlovian behaviorism has morphed into a field of scientific inquiry generally known as *associative learning*. Researchers in this field have developed sophisticated quantitative models of Pavlovian conditioning (Rescorla & Wagner, 1972) and have expanded their domain from simple reflexes to psychiatric disorders related to fear and anxiety (Lissek et al., 2005), drug tolerance and dependence (Siegel, Baptista, Kim, McDonald, & Weise-Kelly, 2000), causal attribution in humans (Shanks, 2007), and many other topics.

A number of approaches to research on learning and behavior have emerged from a radical behaviorist background; together, they constitute the *experimental analysis of behavior*. Radical behaviorism is the main conceptual framework behind *applied behavior analysis*, which is implemented in a broad range of settings and is the standard behavioral treatment for autism spectrum disorder (Matson et al., 2012). The efficacy of immediate and targeted feedback to influence behavior, a key topic in radical behaviorism, informs much of the design of healthcare and lifestyle technologies in the era of mobile devices and gamification (Morford, Witts, Killingsworth, & Alavosius, 2014; Twyman, 2011). The experimental analysis of behavior has yielded techniques for the study of drug-seeking behavior in animal models that are critical for contemporary psychopharmacological research (Banks & Negus, 2012; Spealman & Goldberg, 1978). It has also spawned key mathematical models of learning and behavior (Herrnstein, 1970; Killeen, 1994).

The strength of associative learning and the experimental analysis of behavior are reflected in the organizations and scholarly journals that support modern learning research. Investigators in these fields share their latest findings in the annual meetings of the Pavlovian Society, the Society for the Quantitative Analysis of Behavior, the International Society for Comparative Psychology, and the Comparative Cognition Society, among others. Larger meetings, such as those of the American Psychological Association, the Psychonomic Society, and the Association for Behavior Analysis International, have special tracks for experimental research on learning. Much of this research is published in peer-reviewed journals, such as the *Journal of the Experimental Analysis of Behavior*, the *Journal of Experimental Psychology: Animal Learning & Cognition*, and *Learning & Behavior*.

Modern learning research has had a particularly noticeable impact on the field of *behavioral neuroscience*. This area of research is concerned with the neural basis of behavior, including learning. Learning research and behavioral neuroscience are thus mutually complementary fields. Learning research identifies functional processes whose physiological mechanisms are specified by behavioral neuroscience which, in turn, informs the functional processes that learning scientists study. In this complementary relation, computational and mathematical models often play a critical role. To illustrate this point, consider the Rescorla-Wagner model of learning (Rescorla & Wagner, 1972) (discussed in Chapter 4). This is a mathematical model that explains a wide range of learning effects (also discussed in Chapter 4), one of which is known as *reinforcement learning* (Sutton & Barto, 1998). Among many processes identified by reinforcement learning, one of particular importance is the reduction of prediction error (also identified by the Rescorla-Wagner model). This process guided the search for the neural basis of prediction error, which was eventually found in the phasic activity of dopamine in the dorsal striatum (Lee, Seo, & Jung, 2012; Schultz, 1998). This finding, in turn, has informed theories and models of learning (Maia & Frank, 2011).

ANIMAL SUBJECTS IN BEHAVIORAL RESEARCH

Learning research is, still today, mainly conducted using non-human animals as subjects, primarily rats and mice, but also pigeons, rabbits, hamsters, dogs, and many other species. The rationale behind the preference for animals instead of humans as experimental subjects has not changed much over the last century. Learning is not unique to humans, and the fundamental processes that govern learning processes are shared by many species. For experimental purposes, small animals have some unique advantages. Their environment can be more carefully controlled than the environment of humans, thus minimizing variability in performance that may arise from variability in experience. Under such controlled conditions, animals can be easily motivated to conduct learning tasks that a normal human would find uninteresting. Whereas individual animals may perform a learning task repeatedly with minimal irrelevant variability, human performance is particularly vulnerable to the influence of extraneous factors, including boredom. It is also important to note that, despite the astounding advancement in human brain imaging techniques, there is still no replacement for the direct access to the brain that animal models provide. Thus, investigations on the neural basis of learning are still highly dependent on the use of animal models.

It may be argued that learning researchers should aim at understanding the human experience, including all the complexities that animal models do not capture well. Although the premise of this argument is often true, aiming at a goal does not mean jumping right at it. Physicists trying to understand the motion of objects often use artificial vacuum chambers, and chemists trying to understand how elements react when combined typically conduct their studies in test tubes and beaker flasks, not directly in nature. The basic rationale of experimental research across the sciences is that to understand complex phenomena it is often necessary to break the phenomenon into small, isolatable problems that can be studied under controlled conditions in a laboratory. This approach to problem solving is called *analysis*. To validate analytical solutions, they should demonstrate their utility in nature. This validation is called *synthesis*. In learning research, synthetic validation to experimental findings is typically attained by showing that these findings explain and may impact the behavior of humans in their normal environment (e.g., Vollmer & Bourret, 2000).

The use of animals for experimental purposes raises important ethical concerns. The more extreme challenge to such use comes from viewpoints that disapprove of *any* use of animals by humans.

Although such extreme views are not fully addressed here, it is important to note that they typically ignore that (a) although humans share many basic cognitive capacities with other species, humans and animals differ in cognitive capacities that are key to the notion of personhood, and (b) most humans, with the possible exception of modern urban populations, live and have lived using other species for food, companionship, hunting aids, sources of energy, labor, etc.

Assuming, however, that it is ethical for humans to use other species does not mean that *any* use is necessarily ethical. In the United States, learning research is primarily conducted in universities that are subject to multiple regulations and ethical standards, including those from the Department of Agriculture, Institutional Animal Care and Use Committees (IACUC), funding agencies (e.g., the Office of Laboratory Animal Welfare), scientific organizations (such as the American Psychological Association) (Akins, Panicker, & Cunningham, 2005), and certifications from organizations such as the Association for Assessment and Accreditation of Laboratory Animal Care (AAALAC).

In learning research, some manipulations raise particularly important ethical concerns. To motivate animals to learn a task, they are often presented with stimuli that serve as rewards. Food and water are very effective and practical rewards for food- and water-restricted animals. Food and water restriction are, however, potential challenges to the health and welfare of the animals (Rowland, 2007). *Ad libitum* (i.e., free and constantly available) access to food is also potentially detrimental to the health of animals (Hubert, Laroque, Gillet, & Keenan, 2000)—after all, unlike humans in a grocery store, animals in their natural environment rarely have ad libitum access to food and water. Researchers have devised various protocols that ensure that dietary restriction in laboratory animals keep them healthy and motivated (Toth & Gardiner, 2000).

Although less prevalent than food reward, another form of motivation involves aversive stimuli, typically in the form of a mild (0.17 – 0.80 mA) foot shock. Although foot shock is used to induce stress and depression-like symptoms in animal models (e.g., Naruo, Hara, Nozoe, Tanaka, & Ogawa, 1993), in the context of learning research, such long-term detrimental effects are generally avoided because they are likely to interfere with the learning processes under examination. Aversive stimuli such as a mild foot shock are readily associated with relatively arbitrary stimuli, presumably because of their salience, thus requiring few training trials; under some conditions, even just one trial may suffice for aversive learning to happen (Fanselow, 1990). In any case, it is important to keep in mind that learning researchers have no interest in making their animal subjects sick or weak; instead, they are interested in animals that are healthy and responsive to experimental learning tasks.

REFERENCES

Akins, C. K., Panicker, S. E., & Cunningham, C. L. (2005). *Laboratory animals in research and teaching: Ethics, care, and methods.* Washington, DC: American Psychological Association.

Ashby, F. G., & O'Brien, J. B. (2005). Category learning and multiple memory systems. *Trends in Cognitive Sciences, 9*(2), 83–89.

Banks, M. L., & Negus, S. S. (2012). Preclinical determinants of drug choice under concurrent schedules of drug self-administration. *Advances in pharmacological sciences, 2012*, 281768, 1–18.

Brink, T. (1980). Idiot savant with unusual mechanical ability: An organic explanation. *The American Journal of Psychiatry, 137*(2), 250–251.

Darwin, C. R. (1859). *On the origin of species by means of natural selection, or the preservation of favoured races in the struggle for life.* London, UK: John Murray.

Darwin, C. R. (1872). *The expression of the emotions in man and animals.* London, UK: John Murray.

Day, W. (1983). On the difference between radical and methodological behaviorism. *Behaviorism, 11*(1), 89–102.

Fanselow, M. S. (1990). Factors governing one-trial contextual conditioning. *Animal Learning & Behavior, 18*(3), 264–270.

Gould, S. J., & Lewontin, R. C. (1979). The spandrels of San Marco and the Panglossian paradigm: A critique of the adaptationist programme. *Proceedings of the Royal Society of London B: Biological Sciences, 205*(1161), 581–598.

Herrnstein, R. (1970). On the law of effect. *Journal of the Experimental Analysis of Behavior, 13*(2), 243.

Hubert, M. F., Laroque, P., Gillet, J. P., & Keenan, K. P. (2000). The effects of diet, ad libitum feeding, and moderate and severe dietary restriction on body weight, survival, clinical pathology parameters, and cause of death in control Sprague-Dawley rats. *Toxicological Sciences, 58*(1), 195–207.

Hursh, S. R. (1984). Behavioral economics. *Journal of the Experimental Analysis of Behavior, 42*(3), 435–452.

Killeen, P. R. (1994). Mathematical principles of reinforcement: Based on the correlation of behavior with incentives in short-term memory. *Behavioral and Brain Sciences, 17*, 105–172.

Lee, D., Seo, H., & Jung, M. W. (2012). Neural basis of reinforcement learning and decision making. *Annual Review of Neuroscience, 35*, 287.

Lissek, S., Powers, A. S., McClure, E. B., Phelps, E. A., Woldehawariat, G., Grillon, C., & Pine, D. S. (2005). Classical fear conditioning in the anxiety disorders: A meta-analysis. *Behaviour Research and Therapy, 43*(11), 1391–1424.

Maia, T. V., & Frank, M. J. (2011). From reinforcement learning models to psychiatric and neurological disorders. *Nature Neuroscience, 14*(2), 154–162.

Matson, J. L., Turygin, N. C., Beighley, J., Rieske, R., Tureck, K., & Matson, M. L. (2012). Applied behavior analysis in autism spectrum disorders: Recent developments, strengths, and pitfalls. *Research in Autism Spectrum Disorders, 6*(1), 144–150.

Morford, Z. H., Witts, B. N., Killingsworth, K. J., & Alavosius, M. P. (2014). Gamification: The intersection between behavior analysis and game design technologies. *The Behavior Analyst, 37*(1), 25–40.

Morgan, C. L. (1891). *Animal life and intelligence.* Boston, MA: Ginn & Company.

Naruo, T., Hara, C., Nozoe, S. I., Tanaka, H., & Ogawa, N. (1993). Evaluation of depression in rats exposed to chronic (unpredictable) electric shock. *Pharmacology Biochemistry and Behavior, 46*(3), 667–671.

Pavlov, I. P. (1927). *Conditioned reflexes: An investigation of the physiological activity of the cerebral cortex.* New York, NY: Dover.

Rescorla, R. A., & Wagner, A. R. (1972). A theory of Pavlovian conditioning. In A. Black & W. Prokasy (Eds.), *Classical conditioning, II* (pp. 64–99). New York, NY: Appleton-Century-Crofts.

Rowland, N. E. (2007). Food or fluid restriction in common laboratory animals: Balancing welfare considerations with scientific inquiry. *Comparative Medicine, 57*(2), 149–160.

Schultz, W. (1998). Predictive reward signal of dopamine neurons. *Journal of Neurophysiology, 80*(1), 1–27.

Shanks, D. R. (2007). Associationism and cognition: Human contingency learning at 25. *The Quarterly Journal of Experimental Psychology, 60*(3), 291–309.

Siegel, S., Baptista, M. A., Kim, J. A., McDonald, R. V., & Weise-Kelly, L. (2000). Pavlovian psychopharmacology: The associative basis of tolerance. *Experimental and Clinical Psychopharmacology, 8*(3), 276–293.

Skinner, B. F. (1935). Two types of conditioned reflex and a pseudo type. *The Journal of General Psychology, 12*(1), 66–77.

Skinner, B. F. (1938). *The behavior of organisms: An experimental analysis.* New York, NY: Appleton-Century-Crofts.

Skinner, B. F. (1950). Are theories of learning necessary? *Psychological Review, 57*(4), 193–216.

Skinner, B. F. (1953). *Science and human behavior.* New York, NY: Macmillan.

Spealman, R. D., & Goldberg, S. R. (1978). Drug self-administration by laboratory animals: Control by schedules of reinforcement. *Annual Review of Pharmacology and Toxicology, 18*(1), 313–339.

Sutton, R., & Barto, A. (1998). *Reinforcement learning: An introduction.* Cambridge, MA: MIT Press.

Talmi, D., Seymour, B., Dayan, P., & Dolan, R. J. (2008). Human Pavlovian–instrumental transfer. *The Journal of Neuroscience, 28*(2), 360–368.

Thorndike, E. L. (1911). *Animal intelligence: Experimental studies.* New York, NY: Macmillan.

Toth, L. A., & Gardiner, T. W. (2000). Food and water restriction protocols: Physiological and behavioral considerations. *Journal of the American Association for Laboratory Animal Science, 39*(6), 9–17.

Twyman, J. S. (2011). Emerging technologies and behavioral cusps: A new era for behaviour analysis. *European Journal of Behavior Analysis, 12*(2), 461–482.

Vollmer, T. R., & Bourret, J. (2000). An application of the matching law to evaluate the allocation of two- and three-point shots by college basketball players. *Journal of Applied Behavior Analysis, 33*(2), 137–150.

Watson, J. B. (1913). Psychology as the behaviorist views it. *Psychological Review, 20*(2), 158–177.

Yeomans, M. R. (2006). The role of learning in development of food preferences. In R. Shepherd & M. Raats (Eds.), *The psychology of food choice* (Vol. 3, pp. 93–112). Oxfordshire, UK: CABI.

Image Credits

KEY CONCEPTS

2

FUNDAMENTAL TERMS

Environment vs. organism. Any learning situation comprises a set of components. To identify those components, recall our example of a learning situation from Chapter 1: Ben learning to ride a bicycle without training wheels. There are at least two components to this situation: (1) the bicycle (without training wheels) that Ben is riding and (2) Ben riding it. The first component refers to the physical environment with which Ben is interacting (we can also include here the road over which the bicycle tires roll, maybe a parent watching over Ben, etc.) These are all the things in the situation that are not Ben. The rest of the situation is, of course, Ben himself. To put it more generally, all learning situations can be broken up into two components: an *environment* and an *organism* (Figure 2.1).

Review your example from Box 1.1. What constitutes the environment in that example? What is the organism? Include your answers in Box 2.1 (next page).

Stimulus vs. response. Any of the elements that make up the environment in a learning situation may interact with the organism. The handlebar may pull left or right, and the wheels may turn faster or slower; these aspects of the environment are likely to influence Ben's behavior. We call these aspects of the environment that may elicit a response

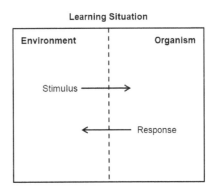

Figure 2.1. Generic representation of a learning situation. The situation is partitioned into two components: an environment and an organism. Aspects of the environment that interact with the organism are called *stimuli*. Aspects of the organism that interact with the environment are called *responses*.

Box 2.1

Environment:

Organism:

from an organism, *stimuli* (singular: stimulus). The voice of an encouraging parent, the temperature of the air—they constitute stimuli in our illustrative learning situation because Ben may respond to them while learning to ride his bicycle.

What, then, is a *response*? It may appear circular, but just like stimuli are defined in terms of their capacity to elicit responses, responses are defined in terms of their elicitation by a stimulus. More precisely, a response is an aspect of the behavior of an organism elicited by a stimulus. Ben pushing his bicycle's pedal, keeping his balance, screaming, etc., constitute responses in our illustrative learning situation, to the extent that they are elicited by stimuli.

The definitions of stimulus and response are not circular, but they are interdependent. To identify a stimulus in a learning situation, it is necessary to identify the potential responses to that stimulus; to identify a response, it is necessary to identify the potential stimuli that elicited that response. Going back again to Box 1.1, identify one stimulus (call it *S*), its potential responses, and, for one of those responses, (call it *R*) its potential stimuli.

Box 2.2

Stimulus S: Potential Responses to Stimulus S:

Response R: Potential Stimuli to Response R:

Learning and conditioning. Let's use the definitions of stimulus and response to further specify what we mean by *learning* and *conditioning*. In Chapter 1, learning was defined as the acquisition by an individual organism, through experience, of the disposition to perform, given the appropriate testing conditions, a specific behavior. This definition implies that learning involves a change in the probability that a stimulus will elicit a response in a particular organism.

The particular type of experience that leads to a change in the probability of a stimulus eliciting a response defines the type of learning taking place. These types of learning are the subject matter of this book.

The definition of conditioning offered in Chapter 1 makes explicit reference to stimuli and responses: It is defined as an experimental training procedure in which an organism is exposed to a particular arrangement of stimuli, and that arrangement causes a particular response to some of those stimuli in future exposures. The particular *arrangement of* stimuli defines the type of learning that results from—and may be studied through—conditioning. Such arrangement, and the demonstration of its causal role over performance, can only be attained through experimental control.

THE DESIGN OF A CONDITIONING EXPERIMENT

Variables

The logic of an experiment is relatively straightforward: To demonstrate that A (say, this switch) causes B (turns off the lights), the experimenter must have control over A (be able to flip the switch up and down) and show that when A changes in a particular way (the switch is flipped down), B happens. It is important to highlight that a correlation between changes in A and B is not sufficient to demonstrate that A causes B (you may have heard the expression *correlation does not imply causation*; well, it is true). Consider, for instance, the correlation between changes in a barometer (which measures atmospheric pressure) and changes in the amount of rainfall. Although a low reading in a barometer often precedes rainfall, it does not cause rainfall; if that were the case, breaking the barometer to force a low reading would result in rain. Causation is demonstrated by turning on and off the presumed cause and showing its effect.

More technically, causation is demonstrated by varying an *independent variable* (IV) and showing its effect on a *dependent variable* (DV). A variable is simply an aspect of the world that may take more than one value. The position of the switch can be up or down, the reading in the barometer can be 940 or 1050 millibars. The IV is the one that the experimenter *manipulates* (e.g., the position of the switch). The DV is the one that the experimenter *measures* (e.g., whether the light is on or off).

There is a third type of variable that is just as important in an experimental design: the *confounding variable*. These are variables that may be correlated with the IV and may cause changes in the DV. In the switch-light experiment, for example, if instead of just flipping one switch we flipped two, A1 and A2, we would not be able to infer that flipping down switch A1 turned off the light, because flipping down A2 could have also turned off the light. In this case, we say that the effects of flipping down A1 and A2 on the light are *confounded*; the position of switch A2 is a confounding variable. To infer that it is A1 that turns off the light and not A2, it is necessary to break the correlation between the position of A1 and A2. In other words, an adequate experimental design *controls* potentially confounding variables, such as the position of A2 in this example.

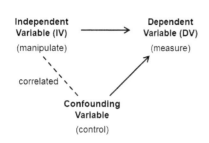

Figure 2.2. Variables in an experimental design. The terms in parentheses indicate the actions that an experimenter must take on each variable to infer causation.

Figure 2.2 is a schematic diagram of the three types of variables involved in an experiment. The experimenter manipulates the IV to cause a measurable change in the DV; because this change may also be caused by a confounding variable, the experimenter controls potentially confounding variables.

Let's use another example, this one more closely related to learning, for an exercise. A rat (call it Rat 1) experiences a single mild foot shock in a test chamber, while another rat (call it Rat 2) is left undisturbed in its home cage. On a test day, both rats are individually placed in the test chamber; Rat 1 does not move ("freezes"), while Rat 2 moves around normally. The experimenter concludes that experiencing mild foot shock in the test chamber made Rat 1 freeze. What is the IV in this example? What is the DV? What values can they take? What confounding variables are potentially involved in this experiment?

Box 2.3

Independent variable (IV):   Values the IV can take:

Dependent variable (DV):   Values the DV can take:

Potentially confounding variables:

In case you were not able to identify a confounding variable in this experiment, here is a hint: Rat 2 not only did not experience the mild foot shock in the test chamber, it did not experience any mild foot shock or have any experience with the test chamber prior to the test. How would you change the design to control these confounding variables?

Box 2.4

Designing a Conditioning Experiment

By now it should be clear that every experiment involves a comparison: Measurements of the DV under one value of the IV are compared to measurements of the DV under other values of the IV. In the light switch example, whether the light is on or off is verified when the switch is down and when the switch is up. This comparison involves at least two situations, one that is called the *experimental condition* and another that is called the *control condition*. The target effect of the IV on the DV is expected under the experimental condition but not under the control condition. To minimize the effect of potentially confounding variables, the experimental and control conditions should be as similar as possible in all respects, except for the value of the IV. Only then can changes in the DV be attributed to changes in the IV.

In the mild foot shock experiment, Rat 1 (the one that experiences the foot shock in the test chamber) is in the experimental condition; Rat 2 is in the control condition. Freezing during the test is expected in Rat 1, not in Rat 2. Although the test results are in agreement with expectations, note that the experimental and control conditions vary in more than one respect. To appreciate this, the IV must be defined as precisely as possible. If the purpose of the experiment is to demonstrate conditioning, this means that freezing results from exposure to a particular arrangement of stimuli. Such exposure is, thus, the IV. In the experimental condition, rats are exposed to a particular arrangement of stimuli; in the control condition they are not. What is, then, this particular arrangement of stimuli? It is, presumably, the presentation of foot shock in the test chamber. So what does it mean to not present this arrangement, while keeping all else as similar as possible as the experimental condition? It means presenting the foot shock, placing the rat in the test chamber, but not presenting the foot shock *in* the test chamber. Typically, Rats 1 and 2 would each be placed in two distinct test chambers (C1 and C2); during training, shock would be delivered in C1 but not in C2 for Rat 1, and in C2 but not in C1 for Rat 2, and a test would then be conducted in C1, showing that Rat 1, but not Rat 2 freezes in C1. Note that in this design (illustrated in Figure 2.3) both rats had equal experience with foot shock and C1 (and also with C2), but only Rat 1 experienced foot shock in C1.

There are two types of conditioning experiments: those focused on learning and those focused on performance. Let's briefly review the distinction between learning and performance again. Whereas

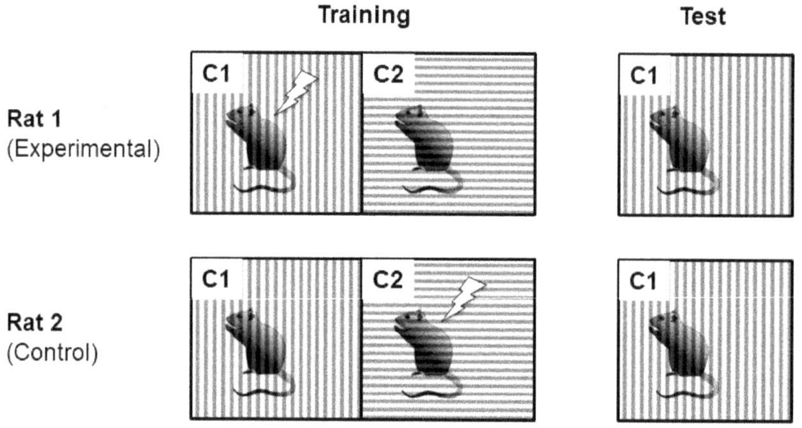

Training **Test**

Rat 1
(Experimental)

Rat 2
(Control)

Figure 2.3. Illustrative foot shock ("fear") conditioning experiment. Rats 1 (experimental) and 2 (control) are exposed to foot shock (yellow lightning bolt) in one of two different chambers, C1 and C2. A test for freezing is conducted for both rats in chamber C1; more freezing by Rat 1 than by Rat 2 would demonstrate conditioning.

learning involves the acquisition of a disposition to behave in a particular way, performance involves the execution of a test, which may or may not reveal an underlying disposition. Having a disposition to stop your car at stop signs does not mean that you will stop at every stop sign: The stop sign may not be visible because of an overgrown tree or heavy rain, or you may be in an emergency. A conditioning experiment focused on learning is one that aims at demonstrating that training yields learning (i.e., that you have acquired a disposition to stop at stop signs). A conditioning experiment focused on performance is one that aims at demonstrating that training conditions determine performance (i.e., that you actually stop at stop signs). Although the difference between these types of conditioning experiments is subtle, it is very important. By addressing different questions, these types of experiments complement each other.[1]

Conditioning Experiments Focused on Learning

A general design of conditioning experiments that are focused on learning is shown in Table 2.1. During training, experimental subjects are exposed to a stimulus arrangement to which control subjects are not exposed. These arrangements will yield responses, but those are not of central interest to infer learning. During testing, experimental and control subjects are exposed to the *same* test stimuli (C1 in the foot shock example; Figure 2.3). To the extent that experimental training yields learning, subjects that underwent experimental training will display a stronger target response than those that underwent control training.

CONDITION	TRAINING	TEST
Experimental	S: Arrangement present R: Not interesting	S: Test arrangement R: Stronger target response
Control	S: Arrangement absent R: Not interesting	S: Test arrangement R: Weaker target response

Table 2.1. General design of conditioning experiments that are focused on learning. "S" stands for stimuli presented and "R" for response measured.

---

1 It is worth noting that each type of conditioning experiment is the main tool of a different tradition in learning research. Whereas conditioning experiments focused on learning are the main tool of associative learning research, those focused on performance are the main tool of the experimental analysis of behavior (see Chapter 1).

In the foot shock example, only one rat was assigned to the experimental condition and one rat was assigned to the control condition. Because the effects of training on learning are variable, these effects are more clearly visible in the average performance of multiple subjects during test. Thus, typical experimental designs assign multiple rats to each condition, typically 6 to 20 per condition, depending on the expected reliability of the training. Subjects are, ideally, assigned randomly to each condition;[2] subjects in each condition constitute a *group* (i.e., experimental group vs. control group).

The experimental design suggested so far is called a *between-subject* design because the average performance of one group is compared against the average performance of another group. Alternatively, subjects may be trained under experimental and control conditions and may also be tested under both conditions. In the design depicted in Figure 2.3, this would involve adding a test in C2 for both experimental and control rats. The critical comparison in this design is not between groups tested under identical conditions, but within groups tested under different conditions (e.g., C1 vs. C2). In this design, the labels "experimental" and "control" no longer apply to Rats 1 and 2 in Figure 2.3; both rats undergo both experimental (foot shock) and control (no foot shock) conditions. In Figure 2.3, the assignment of experimental training to C1 for some rats and to C2 to other rats illustrates a key point in a *within-subject* design: stimulus counterbalancing. If Rat 2 were excluded from the experiment, freezing of Rat 1 in C1 but not in C2 could be due to (a) previously receiving foot shock in C1 but not in C2, or (b) the physical characteristics that distinguish C1 from C2. In other words, in a within-subject design without Rat 2, the IV (receiving foot shock or not) would be confounded with the physical characteristics of the chamber. Counterbalancing the chamber that is paired with foot shock precludes such confounding.

When carefully implemented, within-subject designs have at least two advantages over between-subject designs: First, within-subject experiments demonstrate learning in the individual organism, instead of inferring it from differences between group averages. This is important because learning, by definition, involves changes in the behavior of individual organisms. Second, because conditioning effects are shown in each individual subject, within-subject experiments typically require fewer subjects than between-subject experiments.

Conditioning Experiments Focused on Performance

A general design of conditioning experiments that are focused on performance is shown in Table 2.2. Unlike the standard design of experiments focused on learning, those focused on performance typically use a single, small group of subjects to demonstrate that training conditions control performance. This is accomplished by implementing a design known as a *multiple baseline*. In the simplest multiple baseline design, known as ABA, a training condition A is first implemented, then a training condition B is implemented, and then training condition A is implemented again. Other multiple baseline designs

TRAINING CONDITION A	TRAINING CONDITION B	TRAINING CONDITION A
S: Arrangement A	S: Arrangement B	S: Arrangement A
R: Target response A	R: Target response B	R: Target response A

Table 2.2. General design of conditioning experiments that are focused on performance. "S" stands for stimuli presented, and "R" for response measured.

---

2 Under some circumstances, subjects are assigned manually, equating some pre-training measure across groups. For instance, in human learning experiments, it is ideal to equate gender, age, and other demographic variables before assigning participants to one condition or another.

involve more alternations between training conditions (e.g., ABABA), or more conditions that alternate (e.g., ABCABC). To the extent that training controls performance, the responses in condition A are expected to differ from responses in condition B and are also expected to be recovered on each instantiation of condition A.

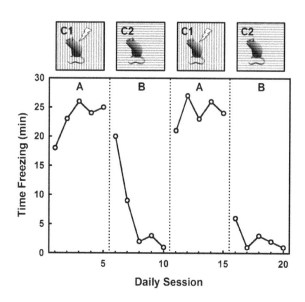

Figure 2.4. Design of a conditioning experiment focused on performance. Condition A (foot shock) is implemented in C1, whereas Condition B (no foot shock) is implemented in C2, following an ABAB design. Hypothetical data are included below, showing amount of time freezing in Conditions A and B.

To illustrate this design, consider again the foot shock experiment. The experiment focused on learning asked the question, "Did the rats learn the association between chamber and foot shock?" Suppose now that we asked a slightly different question: "Did the chamber acquire control over the freezing response?" (Note that the first question is about learning, whereas the second is about performance). To answer this latter question, we design two training conditions: In Condition A, rats are introduced to a chamber and mild foot shock is delivered a few seconds later; in Condition B, rats are introduced to another chamber and nothing happens. For some rats, C1 and C2 are assigned to Conditions A and B, respectively, and for other rats this assignment is reversed (i.e., condition assignment to chamber is counterbalanced). Five sessions of Condition A are conducted first, then five sessions of Condition B are conducted, then five sessions of Condition A are conducted again, and finally five sessions of Condition B are conducted again (Figure 2.4). To the extent that the chamber associated with foot shock acquires control over the freezing response, rats should eventually display a freezing response before the foot shock is delivered in the first Condition A; this response should disappear in Condition B, should reappear in the second Condition A, and should disappear again in the second Condition B (Figure 2.4).

FUNCTIONAL RELATIONS AND THEIR GRAPHICAL REPRESENTATION

Conditioning involves a functional relation between two variables, IV and DV. This means that when the IV is manipulated, the DV also changes in an orderly fashion. Figure 2.5 illustrates this idea using the results from a foot shock experiment (Habib, Ganea, Katz, & Lamprecht, 2013). In this experiment, a tone was presented right before foot shock to a group of rats (*fear conditioning* group), and was presented separately from foot shock to another group of rats (*safety learning* group).

Changes in the IV (tone-shock pairing; x-axis of Figure 2.5) are related to changes in the DV (freezing time during the test; y-axis). During the tone paired with foot shock (black column in Figure 2.5), rats froze longer than during the tone not paired with foot shock (white column). Because the pairing of tone and foot shock was manipulated and confounding variables were controlled, we may claim that the pairing of tone and foot shock *caused* rats to freeze to that tone. More generally, we may say that freezing was conditioned to tone.

Dependent measures are often presented as means of individual measures. In the data shown in Figure 2.5, for instance, not all the rats froze 60 percent of the time during the tone paired with foot shock; *on average* they froze about 60 percent of the time, but some froze longer and some for less time. The error bars around the mean typically indicate the *standard error of the mean*, or SEM, which is an estimate of the variability of the mean in samples like this. The smaller the SEM, the more confident we should be that a similar sample would yield a similar mean. It is not uncommon, however, to display individual performance data in graphs (e.g., Figure 2.4).

Whereas bar graphs such as Figure 2.5 are well suited to compare test performance in experimental and control groups, line graphs such as Figure 2.4 more adequately track changes in individual performance over time. It is therefore not surprising that research focused on learning favors the use of bar graphs to display test results, whereas research focused on performance favors the use of line graphs to display changes in behavior.

Regardless of how data are represented, graphs are typically arranged with values of the IV expressed in the x-axis, and values of the DV expressed in the y-axis. It is also important to highlight that labels in each axis always include measurement units (e.g., "min," which stands for "minutes," in the y-axis of Figure 2.4).

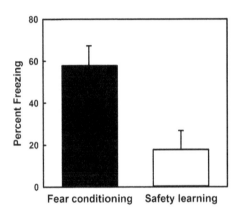

Figure 2.5. Percent of the time freezing in the presence of a tone paired with foot shock (Fear conditioning) vs. a tone not paired with foot shock (Safety learning). From Habib, Ganea, Katz and Lamprecht (2013).

Types of Functions

Empirical and theoretical functions. The functions displayed in Figures 2.4 and 2.5 are *empirical* functions because they track observed data. These functions typically assess the DV only at select values of the IV, either because other values are not possible (e.g., there are no 13.5 days of training in Figure 2.4), or because other values are not considered (e.g., in a drug study, three doses may be tested, 0.1, 0.3, and 0.6 mg/kg; in such case, a 0.2 mg/kg dose is possible in principle, but is not considered). Either way, these functions are *discrete*, because they only include a finite number of values on the x-axis.

Theoretical functions, in contrast, can be continuous. Theoretical functions express predictions (hypotheses) from models and theories, relating expected performance (or processes underlying performance) to an IV. Because these are not actually observed relations, an infinite number of IV values within a range may be considered when constructing a theoretical function. Consider, for instance, the functional relation between the number of pellets of food delivered per minute (the IV) and the number of lever presses emitted per minute to obtain those pellets (the DV). Figure 2.6 shows such empirical function in each of three strains of rat (symbols), along with fitted theoretical functions (curves). The theoretical functions are derived from a model of performance known as the quantitative law of effect (Herrnstein, 1970) (more on this in Chapter 6).

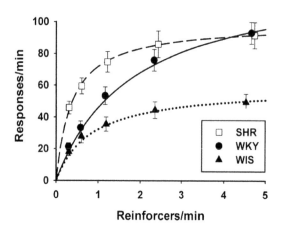

Figure 2.6. Responses (lever presses) per minute as a function of the number of food pellets (reinforcers) per minute, obtained from lever pressing. The symbols represent empirical data obtained from three strains of rat: spontaneously hypertensive rat (SHR), Wistar-Kyoto (WKY), and Wistar (WIS). The curves are theoretical functions based on Herrnstein's (1970) quantitative law of effect, fitted to the data. Adapted from Hill, Herbst, and Sanabria (2012).

Linear functions. Functions, whether discrete or continuous, empirical or theoretical, may take many shapes. Some shapes are particularly interesting because they reveal order in the data and are more easily described in mathematical terms. *Linear functions* are the simplest of these functions; they indicate that any change in the IV yields a proportional change (in the same or in the opposite direction) as in the DV. Linear functions are expressed as straight lines when drawn in *x-y* coordinates. They are expressed mathematically as

$$DV = mIV + b \qquad (2.1)$$

where *m* and *b* are the slope and the y-intercept of the function, respectively. If the DV changes in the same direction of the IV, *m* is positive (Figure 2.7A); if the DV changes in the opposite direction of the IV, *m* is negative (Figure 2.7B). When IV = 0, DV = *b*.

There are many variables that are linearly related. For instance, if you are in a store buying lollipops, the number of lollipops you obtain is linearly related to the amount of money you spend on lollipops, where *m* is positive—it is the reciprocal of the price of each lollipop (*m* = 1/price)—and *b* = 0. If you buy 100 lollipops and you eat them, the number of lollipops left is a linear function of the number of lollipops you have eaten, with *m* = –1 and *b* = 100. In the box, identify two variables that are linearly related; identify the values of *m* and *b*.

Box 2.5

Variable 1 (DV):

Variable 2 (IV):

m =

b =

Negatively ac-celerated functions.
Sometimes the DV does not vary propor-tionally to the IV. For instance, it is not un-common that changes at low values of the IV result in larger changes in the DV than similar changes at high values of the IV. This non-lin-ear relation between IV and DV is a *negatively accelerated function.* The theoretical curves of Figure 2.6 are ex-amples of negatively accelerated functions: The same change in reinforcers per minute yield larger changes in responses per minute when the change starts at a low value of the IV (e.g., zero to 1 rein-forcers/min) than when it starts at a high value (e.g., 4 to 5 reinforcers/min).

Negatively acceler-ated functions are fairly common in learning and conditioning research because they incorporate a limit to

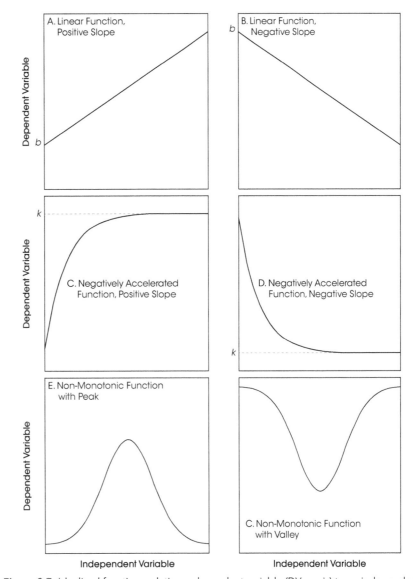

Figure 2.7. Idealized functions relating a dependent variable (DV, *y* axis) to an independent variable (IV, *x* axis), illustrate the various types of functions typical in learning and condition-ing research. **A.** Linear function with positive slope (Equation 2.1 with *m* > 0); *b* is the y-in-tercept, the value of the DV when the IV = 0. **B.** Linear function with negative slope (Equation 2.2 with *m* < 0). **C.** Negatively accelerated function with positive slope; *k* is the asymptote of the function, indicated also by an intermittent gray line. **D.** Negatively accelerated func-tion with negative slope. **E.** Non-monotonic function with a peak. **F.** Non-monotonic function with a valley.

performance. In Figure 2.6, it seems unlikely that responses/min would increase linearly to infinity; no organism can respond infinitely fast. Instead, it appears that responding in each of the three strains gets closer and closer to a rate that they cannot reach, even when reinforcers are plentiful. That rate, for instance, appears to be 50 responses/min for the Wistar strain. That rate (i.e., that value of the DV) is called the *asymptote* of the function.

Some negatively accelerated functions have a positive slope, in which higher values of the IV are as-sociated with higher values of the DV (Figures 2.6 and 2.7C); others have a negative slope (Figure 2.6D). The asymptote of negatively accelerated functions with a negative slope typically prevents the DV from taking negative values, which often does not make sense (e.g., a negative number of responses). For example, the size of an image in your retina is a negatively accelerated function, with a negative slope and an asymptote of zero, of the distance between your eye and the object.

Unlike linear functions, there is no single mathematical expression that can describe all negatively accelerated functions; there are multiple functions that may take a negatively accelerated form. In the example of Figure 2.6, the mathematical expression fitted to the data was the Herrnstein's (1970) quantitative law of effect,

$$DV = \frac{kIV}{IV + R_e} \tag{2.2}$$

where k is the asymptotic response rate (as $IV \rightarrow \infty$, $DV \rightarrow k$), and R_e is inversely proportional to the slope of the function (a lower R_e yields steeper rises toward the asymptote).

In the box, provide an example of two variables that are related by a negatively accelerated function. Is the slope of the function positive or negative? What is the asymptote of the function?

Box 2.6
_____

Variable 1 (DV):

Variable 2 (IV):

Is the slope positive or negative?

Asymptote:

Non-monotonic functions. Linear and negatively accelerated functions are both monotonic. That is, when the value of the IV changes in one direction (increases or decreases), the DV either always increases or always decreases, even if just slightly. In Figure 2.6, as reinforcers/min increase, responses/min always increase, and when reinforcers/min decrease, responses/min always decrease. Not all functions in learning and conditioning are monotonic. In some functions, the DV rises and drops (or vice versa) as the IV changes in one direction; these are *non-monotonic* functions (Figures 2.7E and 2.7F). The peak or valley of those functions typically identifies a key value of the IV where performance is maximal or minimal. For instance, if foot shock were paired with a tone frequency of 8 kHz, and testing was conducted on frequencies ranging between 2 and 24 kHz, the function relating freezing duration (DV) to tone frequency (IV) would likely peak at about 8 kHz.

In the box, provide an example of two variables that are related by a non-monotonic function. Does the function have a peak or a valley? What is the value of the IV (x axis) at the peak or valley?

Box 2.7

Variable 1 (DV):

Variable 2 (IV):

Does the function have a peak or a valley?

Value of the IV at the peak or valley:

REFERENCES

Habib, M. R., Ganea, D. A., Katz, I. K., & Lamprecht, R. (2013). ABL1 in thalamus is associated with safety but not fear learning. *Frontiers in Systems Neuroscience, 7*, 5.

Herrnstein, R. J. (1970). On the law of effect. *Journal of the Experimental Analysis of Behavior, 13*, 243–266.

Hill, J. C., Herbst, K., & Sanabria, F. (2012). Characterizing operant hyperactivity in the Spontaneously Hypertensive Rat. *Behavioral and Brain Functions, 8*, 5.

Image Credits

UNCONDITIONED BEHAVIOR

3

REFLEXES AND MODAL ACTION PATTERNS

Reflexes. Conditioning involves arranging the environment to cause a behavior. Previous examples involved a particular kind of arrangement, regularly presenting one stimulus before a second stimulus, which results in a change in the response to the first stimulus. We call this procedure Pavlovian conditioning. In our example, a sound is presented before meat powder to a dog, making the dog salivate to the sound (Figure 1.2 in Chapter 1), and foot shock is presented in a chamber to a group of rats, making the rats freeze in that chamber (Figure 2.3 in Chapter 2). What is the simplest arrangement of stimuli that would result in a response?

For example, consider what would happen if dust touched your eye. Such stimulus will likely elicit a blinking response. This is called the corneal reflex (Cruccu, Agostino, Berardelli, & Manfredi, 1986). Note that the arrangement to produce a corneal reflex is as simple as it can get: It only involves the presentation of a stimulus. There is, however, no learning involved in a reflex: Your predisposition toward blinking to dust in your eye does not require any experience, only a functioning nervous system. You do not learn to blink to dust, just like you do not learn to sneeze to an irritant in your nose, or to remove your hand from a very hot surface. Reflexes, by definition, are not learned and are not conditioned. Reflexes are thus the simplest form of unconditioned behavior.

Unconditioned behavior may be represented as it is in Figure 3.1. To highlight that the stimulus unconditionally (that is, regardless of experience) produces the response, the stimulus is called an *unconditioned stimulus* (or US), and the response an *unconditioned response* (or UR). These labels also highlight the interdependent nature of stimuli and responses. Blinking is

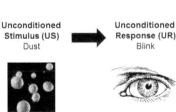

Figure 3.1. Schematic representation of unconditioned behavior, with a blinking response to dust as example.

31

an unconditioned response if an unconditioned stimulus, such as contact with dust, elicits it. If, however, a mild sound warns you that dust is going to be blown into your eye, you would also blink to that sound. Although both blinking responses may be physically identical, their *function* is different. To blink to a sound that warns you of dust, you must have learned that the sound precedes dust, so it is a conditioned response.

Provide three examples of unconditioned behavior, perhaps reflexes, that every healthy adult person is likely to display. Indicate the corresponding US and the UR.

Box 3.1

US 1:   UR 1:

US 2:   UR 2:

US 3:   UR 3:

All animals are equipped with a large number of reflexes from the moment they are born. In humans, these reflexes are classified as either *primitive* or *permanent*. Primitive reflexes typically disappear after the first year of age, whereas permanent reflexes do not go away. Table 3.1 lists a few primitive reflexes that are included in the standard neurological examination of newborn children. The absence of some of these primitive reflexes, or their persistence past certain age, is indicative of neurological disorders (Khan, Garcia-Sosa, Hageman, Msall, & Kelley, 2014; Zafeiriou, 2004). Permanent reflexes in humans include the corneal reflex, the patellar reflex (striking the patellar ligament of the knee produces a kicking response), the pupillary light reflex (light reduces the size of the pupil), coughing, shivering, sneezing, etc. (Aramideh & Ongerboer de Visser, 2002).

Modal action patterns. Unconditioned behavior is not always as simple as a reflex; it often involves complex sequences of actions, which are sometimes coordinated with a conspecific. Consider, for instance, the courtship behavior of the male, three-spined stickleback, a species of fish (Tinbergen & Van Iersel, 1947). In the presence of a pregnant female, the male three-spined stickleback emits a series of sideward movements, punctuated with darting movements toward the female and with sudden stops. In response to this behavior, the female approaches the male and leads it toward a tunnel-shaped nest. She then deposits her eggs in the nest, the male fertilizes them, and he chases

REFLEX	STIMULUS	RESPONSE	AGE AT DISAPPEARANCE
Moro	Rapidly extending head in relation to body	Hand opening, abduction and extension of arms and legs followed by flexion	3–4 months
Asymmetric tonic neck	Turning head to one side	Extension of one arm toward one side of the head while flexing the other arm (fencing posture)	6 months
Palmar grasp	Placing object in palm	Fingers close (grasp)	2–3 months (turns voluntary)
Sucking	Placing object in roof of mouth	Sucking	4 months (turns voluntary)
Rooting	Cheek stroking	Head turning with mouth open in direction of stroking	7 months
Stepping	Sole of foot touching flat surface	Leg flexion and extension in slow stepping action	6 weeks
Plantar	Stroking of external side of sole	Smaller toes fan out and big toe flexes toward shin	12 months
Galant	Stroking of one side of the back while facing down	Flexing of trunk on stroked side	4 months

Table 3.1. **Primitive Neonatal Reflexes**

her away (Figure 3.2). Surprising as it may seem, three-spined sticklebacks do not learn this pattern of responses; it is simply displayed if the appropriate stimulus (a pregnant female) is present, under the appropriate circumstances. Such complex unconditioned patterns of behavior are called *modal action patterns* (Barlow, 1977) (originally called *fixed action patterns*).

Examples of modal action patterns include the mating dance of sage-grouses (Wiley, 1973), egg-retrieval in snow geese (Lank, Bousfield, Cooke, & Rockwell, 1991), and the begging response of young herring gulls (Tinbergen & Perdeck, 1950). These responses have a few features in common. As unconditioned behavior, they are all elicited by a US, which is called the *sign* or *releasing stimulus*. In courtship and mating responses, the sign stimulus is typically a conspecific of the opposite sex. In the egg-retrieval response, where geese roll into the nest eggs that are lying nearby, the sign stimuli are the eggs (or sufficiently similar objects). In the begging response, where newly hatched gulls induce regurgitation in their parents by pecking their bills, the sign stimulus is a red patch in the bill of the parent.

Although modal action patterns are not dependent on prior experience, they are dependent on the

Figure 3.2. Courtship behavior of the male, three-spined stickleback, an example of a model action pattern.

motivational state of the animal. Male three-spine sticklebacks engage in courtship behavior only in spring, their mating season. Geese retrieve eggs only if nesting. Gulls peck their parents' bill only if hungry.

Another defining characteristic of modal action patterns is that once they are initiated they are carried to completion. This can be readily demonstrated in the egg-retrieval behavior of geese. Once a goose starts rolling back an egg into its nest, the egg may be removed and the goose will continue making the movements as if it were rolling an egg into its nest.

Physical variations, generalization, and supernormal stimuli. The efficacy of a releasing stimulus in eliciting a UR depends on the physical properties of that stimulus (Baerends & Kruijt, 1973). For instance, the fish *Haplochromis burtoni*, when in a territorial state, displays a black stripe below its eye, an *eyebar*. Conspecifics respond unconditionally to this eyebar with aggression. However, not all eyebars produce the same aggressive response: Those that are parallel to the forehead elicit more aggression than those that are perpendicular to the forehead (Heiligenberg, Kramer, & Schulz, 1972) (Fig. 3.3).

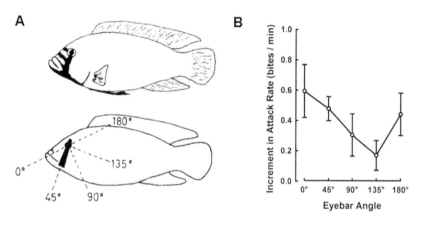

Figure 3.3. **A.** Line representations of a live *Haplochromis burtoni* (top) and an experimental dummy (bottom). The angle of the dummy's eyebar relative to its forehead was experimentally manipulated. **B.** Changes in attack rate as a function of eyebar angle, over a 30-second period (the change was calculated relative to the attack rate elicited by young conspecifics). A 135-degree eyebar (perpendicular to forehead) elicited the fewest attacks. Based on Heiligenberg, et al. (1972).

The angle of the eyebar may be thought of as a variable, insofar as it can take multiple values. More precisely, it may be thought of as an independent variable (IV), to the extent that an experimenter can manipulate it in a fish dummy that elicits an aggressive response in real fish. The rate of attacks that the eyebar elicits would constitute the dependent variable (DV). Figure 3.3B thus shows the functional relation between IV and DV. You may recognize this function from Chapter 2 as a non-monotonic function with a valley. The valley of the function is located at the value of the releasing stimulus (the IV) that elicits the weakest response.

The notion that responses vary with changes in some dimension of a stimulus is not unique to unconditioned behavior. As we will see in the remainder of this book, it is also present across all forms of learning and conditioned behavior (Ghirlanda & Enquist, 2003). This notion is called *stimulus generalization*; the function that represents it is a stimulus generalization *gradient*. A generalization gradient is typically a non-monotonic function, with a peak indicating the value of the stimulus that most effectively elicits the response (e.g., an eyebar parallel to the forehead at 0 degrees or 180 degrees in Figure 3.3), or a valley indicating the value of the stimulus that more effectively suppresses the response. In other words, the idea of stimulus generalization is that progressively larger changes in the stimulus produce progressively larger changes in the response.

The generalization gradient of releasing stimuli does not always peak at values that are normally present in nature. Eyebars parallel to the forehead are very unusual, but they elicit the strongest attacking response in *H. burtoni*. A red patch in the bill of a parent herring gull elicits a begging (pecking) response in its offspring; this, in turn, elicits regurgitation of food in the parent who feeds its offspring. Although natural red patches are effective at eliciting the begging response, increasing their contrast to the background in an artificial stimulus and adding an internal white ring makes them even more effective (Tinbergen & Perdeck, 1950). These artificial but exceedingly effective releasing stimuli are called *supernormal stimuli* (Barrett, 2010). It has been argued that humans regularly manufacture supernatural stimuli to elicit desired responses in others, such as with cosmetics that signal attractiveness (Etcoff, Stock, Haley, Vickery, & House, 2011).

REPEATED PRESENTATIONS OF AN UNCONDITIONED STIMULUS

As long as the organism is healthy and in the appropriate motivational state, the *first* presentation of a US increases the probability of a corresponding UR. Interestingly, *continued* or *repeated* presentation of the same US may change the strength of the corresponding UR. There is a broad range of behaviors that show this effect. In the territorial male *H. burtoni*, for instance, repeated presentations of a male conspecific increases its aggressiveness (Heiligenberg & Kramer, 1972). Stressful situations elicit a secretion of corticosterone from adrenal glands, but such secretion is reduced with continued stress (Pitman, Ottenweller, & Natelson, 1988). In fact, whether the repeated presentation of a US weakens or strengthens a UR sometimes depends on the context in which it is repeatedly presented. Consider, for instance, the *acoustic startle response* of rats. When a loud sound is suddenly presented to a rat, it elicits a quick jumping response. If the sound is repeatedly presented in a quiet environment, the startle response is progressively weakened; if, however, the sound is repeatedly presented in a noisy or fearful environment, the startle response becomes stronger (Davis, 1974; Koch & Schnitzler, 1997). This context-dependent weakening or potentiation of the acoustic startle response is also observed in humans, and it has important implications for psychopathology (Cadenhead, Carasso, Swerdlow, Geyer, & Braff, 1999; Grillon, Ameli, Woods, Merikangas, & Davis, 1991).

Behavioral sensitization and cross-sensitization. The increase in responding due to the repeated stimulation is known as *behavioral sensitization* (Peeke & Petrinovich, 1984). This effect is generally attributed to an increase in arousal that accumulates with repeated presentations of the US (Groves & Thompson, 1970; Thompson, 2009). Because this increase in arousal is experience-dependent and does not involve a change in sensorimotor capacity, it qualifies as a (very simple) form of learning, which is referred to as *non-associative learning* (non-associative because it involves only one stimulus, the US). In fact, sensitization implies a rudimentary form of memory because, for a response to strengthen, the organism must somehow remember the previous presentations of the sensitized stimulus.

Increased arousal affects multiple responses, which implies that sensitization is not stimulus-specific. For instance, repeated presentations of foot-shock not only sensitizes pain responses in rats, but also sensitizes acoustic startle responses (Davis, 1989). Painful stimuli, in general, show similar properties (Weyer et al., 2016). Drugs, particularly psychostimulants, may also produce relatively minor effects on behavior and mood that sensitize with repeated administration (Strakowski, Sax, Setters, & Keck, 1996); they may also sensitize the effect of other drugs (Itzhak & Martin, 1999). The increased response to one stimulus due to the repeated presentation of another stimulus is known as *sensitization generalization*, or *cross-sensitization*.

Sensory adaptation and motor fatigue. Whereas sensitization appears to reflect only an increase in arousal, a wider range of mechanisms appears to underlie the decline in response due to repeated stimulation. In fact, this response decline may or may not be stimulus-specific. To examine the mechanisms that underlie these effects, consider again the acoustic-startle example. For the sound to produce a startle response in its first presentation, the rat must be able to hear the sound and produce the startling response. The repeated presentation of the sound could thus reduce the startle response in at least two ways: by reducing the capacity to hear the sound, or by reducing the capacity to produce the startling response. More generally, the repeated presentation of the US may reduce the sensory capacity to detect the US (because of changes in sensory receptors), or may reduce the capacity to produce the UR (because of its repeated production). The former is known as *sensory adaptation* and the latter as *motor fatigue* (Rankin et al., 2009). Although sensory adaptation and motor fatigue involve experience-dependent changes in behavior, they do not qualify as learning; rather, they fall in the category of changes in sensorimotor capacity (Figure 1.1 in Chapter 1).

Sensory adaptation occurs, for instance, with the continued presentation of olfactory and visual stimuli (De Palo et al., 2013; Kleene, 2008; Laughlin, 1989). Photoreceptors in the retina adapt to the continued presentation of light in a particular color, yielding weaker responses to that color and the illusory effect of an afterimage (Ware, 1980). Similarly, motor fatigue occurs with the repeated exertion of a muscle. For example, the repeated exertion of the calf muscle reduces its reflexive response to electrical stimulation (Garland & McComas, 1990).

A key feature of sensory adaptation and motor fatigue is that they reduce responding in a non-stimulus-specific manner. If red-sensitive photoreceptors are continually stimulated, responsiveness to red stimuli projected in the same location of the retina will diminish, regardless of any other feature of the stimulus. If the calf muscle is fatigued, any reflex that uses that muscle will be reduced, regardless of the nature of the stimulus that elicits that reflex. Nonetheless, repeated stimulation may reduce responding through a third mechanism that, unlike all mechanisms considered so far, is stimulus-specific, and, like sensitization, involves learning. It is called *behavioral habituation* (Rankin et al., 2009).

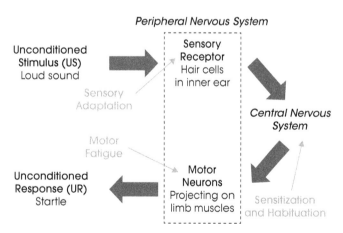

Figure 3.4. Changes in unconditioned response (UR) after multiple presentations of an unconditioned stimulus (US), illustrated with the acoustic startle response. The US (e.g., a loud sound) activates a sensory receptor in the peripheral nervous system (e.g., hair cells in the inner ear), which may adapt. The sensory receptor sends a signal to the central nervous system, which is the site of non-associative learning processes (sensitization and habituation). A signal is then sent to motor neurons (which may project to limb muscles), resulting in a UR (e.g., a startle response).

Behavioral habituation. The stimulus-specific decline in response due to the repeated presentation of a stimulus, and that is caused neither by sensory adaptation nor by motor fatigue, is called behavioral habituation. Because, like sensitization, habituation is experience-dependent and does not involve a reduced sensorimotor capacity, it qualifies as non-associative learning. Also like sensitization, habituation is dependent on processes taking place in the central, instead of the peripheral, nervous system (Figure 3.4). There are many unconditioned behaviors that habituate, including the acoustic-startle response in humans (Cadenhead et al., 1999) and rats (Koch & Schnitzler, 1997), stress-induced secretion of corticosterone (Pitman et al., 1988), and salivation elicited by food-related odors (Epstein et al., 2003).

An experiment on infant visual perception illustrates the notion of stimulus specificity in habituation (McKenzie, Tootell, & Day, 1980). In this experiment, five- to seven-month-old infants were exposed repeatedly to a colored model of an adult female head. For a group of infants (Control), the model was large and presented at a distance of 60 cm from the infant. For another group (Farther), the model was also large, but presented closer, at 30 cm. For a third group (Larger), the

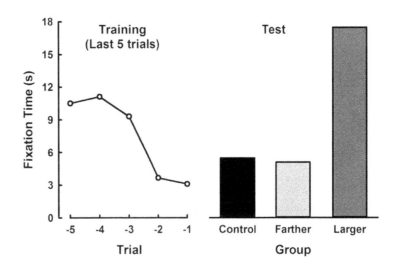

Figure 3.5. Habituation of a fixation response to a model of a female head. The curve shows the pooled mean fixation time of all groups—each trained on a different stimulus—during the last five training trials. The bars are the test performance of each group using the Control stimulus. Based on McKenzie et al. (1980), Experiment 1.

model was small and was presented at 60 cm. The DV in this experiment was the amount of time that the infant fixated on the model stimulus. After the fixation time was shorter than a criterion, all groups were tested with a large model at 60 cm, identical to the one presented to the Control group. Therefore, because each group was trained with a different stimulus, testing with the same stimulus effectively moved it farther away for group Farther, was made larger for group Larger, and did not change for group Control. The results of this experiment are shown in Figure 3.5. Mean fixation time declined below four seconds, with repeated presentations of the same stimulus. When the same stimulus was presented during the test (Control), fixation time increased only slightly, to about five to six seconds. When the test was conducted on a larger model (Larger), fixation time increased substantially, to about 17 to 18 seconds. This difference in test performance shows the specificity of habituation to the model: Once the size of the model was changed, the UR was recovered.

Generalization of habituation. Fig. 3.5 shows another interesting effect (or rather, lack thereof): When the test was conducted on a model located farther away from the infant (Farther), performance was virtually identical to Control infants. The similarity of test performance in groups Control and Farther illustrates the notion of stimulus generalization of habituated behavior. In unconditioned behavior, generalization is described as progressively larger changes in the stimulus that produce progressively larger changes in the response. When applied to habituated behavior, it may be described as progressively larger changes in the *test* stimulus (relative to the habituated stimulus) that produce progressively stronger responses.

Habituation generalization gradients can be generated using, as test stimuli, variations of the habituated stimulus over a sensory dimension. Rubel and Rosenthal (1975), for instance, constructed such a generalization gradient around a habituated 1000-Hz tone in one- and nine- to ten-day-old chicks, using the eye-opening response to sound (Figure 3.6). Chicks normally keep their eyes closed but open them when a sound is presented. The eye-opening response habituates with repeated presentations of the sound, but responding to the test stimulus recovers as the training and test stimuli differ.

Generalization of habituation over physically similar stimuli, such as 1000 and 1050 Hz in one-day-old chicks (Figure 3.6), is rather unsurprising. It suggests, however, something important about the

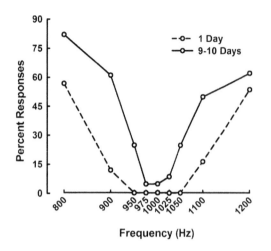

Figure 3.6. Generalization gradient of a habituated 1000-Hz tone in one-day and nine- to ten-day old chicks. The curves show mean percent of eye-opening responses to each of seven test tones, ranging from 800 to 1200 Hz. The weakest response was observed near the habituated 1000-Hz frequency. Based on Rubel and Rosenthal (1975), Experiment 2.

sensory acuity of the organism. Figure 3.6 shows, for instance, that whereas one-day-old chicks treat 950- to 1050-Hz tones as if they were the same, such range is narrowed when they are nine to ten days old. Narrower generalization gradients indicate higher sensory acuity. The enhancement of auditory acuity in chicks within the first few days after hatching, suggests that brain structures responsible for hearing continue developing after hatching.

More surprising, perhaps, is the generalization of habituation across stimuli that are distinguishable. Although with habituation to a head model 30 cm away generalized to a model 60 cm away (Figure 3.5), it is unlikely that infants cannot detect such change in stimulus location. It is more likely that what controls the fixation response is not the distance to the stimulus (within a range), but other features related to the head itself, such as its size, shape, color, etc. This seems adaptive, particularly if the fixation response helps the infant distinguish between individuals of varying importance to him or her (e.g., parents vs. strangers). It is probably adaptive for six-month-old infants to respond similarly to the same individual regardless of the distance to them, and despite the change in the visual field of the infant.

The stimulus-specificity of habituation may be exploited to assess sensory acuity across a wide range of species if a careful experimental design is implemented. More generally, habituated behavior allows researchers to study how organisms perceive the world, particularly when they cannot provide verbal reports. For instance, using this tool, researchers have shown evidence that dogs can perceive human action as goal directed (Marshall-Pescini, Ceretta, & Prato-Previde, 2014), and three-month-old infants can discriminate between emotional expressions in familiar faces (Walker-Andrews, Krogh-Jespersen, Mayhew, & Coffield, 2011).

Now consider the examples of unconditioned behavior that you listed in Box 3.1. Select one of your examples and indicate what would be the effect of repeated presentations of the US on the UR. Would it sensitize? Would it habituate? Would it decline in strength because of sensory adaptation or motor fatigue? Briefly explain.

Box 3.2

INVESTIGATING NON-ASSOCIATIVE LEARNING

Behavioral sensitization and habituation constitute non-associative learning because they involve a change in the predisposition to behave in a particular way (the UR becomes weaker or stronger) as a result of a particular experience (the repeated presentation of the US). The non-associative aspect of sensitization and habituation implies that these changes in behavior do not constitute conditioning: They involve no arrangement of stimuli, other than the repeated presentation of a single one.

Characterizing habituation and sensitization as learning processes implies that, like all other learning phenomena, they may only be demonstrated experimentally. As in any other experiment, we must first identify an independent variable (IV, the one that is experimentally manipulated), a dependent variable (DV, the one that is measured), and potentially confounding variables (which should be controlled for) (Figure 2.2). Based on the definition of behavioral habituation and sensitization, the IV in a habituation/sensitization experiment is the number of presentations of the US, which can go from zero to any positive number. The DV is the dimension of the UR that is expected to be sensitive to the IV, such as the fixation time in infants (measured in, say, seconds), the levels of plasma corticosterone (measured in, say, ng/ml), or mood ratings (measured using a Likert scale). Often times, the key DV is not a level, amount, or rating, which may take many values, but is whether or not the US elicits the UR. For instance, after a presentation of the startling sound, the acoustic-startle response either occurs or it does not occur—either the human participant blinks or does not, and either the rat jumps or it does not. Instead of a range of values, these DVs can only take two values: The UR is either elicited or it is not. In such cases, the typical DV is the proportion of presentations of the US that elicit the UR (e.g., the proportion of presentations of the sound that results in a startling response); this is sometimes called the *probability* of the UR, given the US.

The rationale of non-associate learning experiments is very similar to that of a conditioning experiment focused on learning (Table 2.1). At least two conditions are necessary, an experimental condition and a control condition. Each condition assumes a different value of the IV. In a typical habituation/sensitization experiment, the experimental condition consists of multiple presentations of the US, whereas the control condition consists of no presentations of the US. The effect of variations in the IV is then assessed in a common test.

The McKenzie et al. (1980) study on visual constancy in infants is an example of a habituation experiment that is well designed. In that study, two IVs were examined: the size of the model (Larger vs. Control) and the distance of the model (Farther vs. Control). After training under one value or another of each IV, habituation was tested by measuring the fixation time—the DV—under identical (Control) conditions. By following this design, differences in the DV during the test could only be attributed to changes in the IV during training.

Design of a sensitization experiment. Although they follow a similar rationale, slightly different experimental designs are required to demonstrate sensitization and habituation because sensitization is not stimulus-specific and habituation is. Table 3.2 shows a general

CONDITION	TRAINING	SENSITIZATION TEST
Experimental	A	S: A
Control	Not A	R: EXP > CTRL

Table 3.2. General design of a sensitization experiment. Stimulus A is presented in the experimental condition but not in the control condition. The test stimulus (S) is A. Stronger responding to A in the Experimental condition than in the Control condition would demonstrate sensitization of A [R(Sensitization): EXP > CTRL].

design for a sensitization experiment. Subjects are either exposed to the US (indicated in Table 3.2 by the letter A) or they are not (Not A). This is necessarily a between-subject design, because a subject in the experimental condition, experiencing A, cannot be in the control condition, not experiencing A. All subjects are then exposed to the same test: a presentation of A. If A were sensitized, Experimental subjects would respond more to A than Control subjects.

It is important to notice that the test in Table 3.2 is the first encounter of the Control subjects with A, just as the first training trial is the first encounter of the Experimental subjects with A. This implies that responsiveness to A of the Control subjects during the test should be similar to the responsiveness of the Experimental subjects at the beginning of training. It is important to verify this similarity because it means that the groups only differ in their training, not in their initial responsiveness to A, so differences in test performance can be safely attributed to differences in training.

Design of a habituation experiment. If the design in Table 3.2 were implemented, and instead of EXP > CTRL the result was EXP < CTRL, it would be tempting to conclude that A was habituated. Such a result, however, would not rule out sensory adaptation or motor fatigue. A more adequate design for a habituation experiment—one that rules out sensory adaptation and motor fatigue—is described in Table 3.3. This design includes two stimuli, A and B, both of which elicit the UR similarly. During training, Experimental subjects are exposed to A, whereas Control subjects are exposed to B (here the "Experimental" vs. "Control" assignment is arbitrary). The test consists of presenting A and B separately to all subjects. If the trained stimulus were habituated, Experimental subjects would respond less to A and more to B than Control subjects (Figure 3.7). Similar to the design for sensitization, initial responsiveness to A and B should be compared across groups to rule out their contribution to differences in test performance.

CONDITION	TRAINING	HABITUATION TEST
Experimental	A	S: A / B
Control	B	R: A: EXP < CTRL
		B: EXP > CTRL

Table 3.3. General design of a habituation experiment. Stimulus A is presented in the Experimental condition, whereas stimulus B is presented in the control condition. During the test, stimuli A and B are presented separately, as indicated by the slash (/). Stronger response to A in the Experimental condition, and stronger response to B in the control condition, would demonstrate habituation of A for the Experimental group, and of B for the control group.

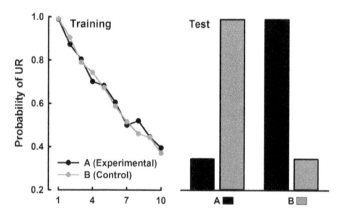

Figure 3.7. Expected results from a habituation experiment, following the design of Table 3.3. During training, the first exposure to A and B elicits a very strong UR in the Experimental (black) and Control (gray) subjects, respectively. As A and B are repeatedly presented during training, the URs weaken. During the test, A elicits a weaker UR in Experimental subjects than in Control subjects (left columns); B elicits a stronger UR in Experimental subjects than in Control subjects (right columns). Notice that test responsiveness to A in Control subjects and to B in Experimental subjects is just as high as the responsiveness to A in Experimental subjects and to B in Control subjects on the first training trial.

Notice how the two-stimulus design controls for sensory adaptation and motor fatigue. The key is that A and B elicit the same UR. In Figure 3.7, the high responsiveness to B in Experimental subjects indicates that their low responsiveness to A was not due to motor fatigue, because these subjects were still capable of producing the UR. To the extent that A and B are in the same sensory modality and impinge on the same sensory receptors, the high responsiveness to B in Experimental subjects indicates that their low responsiveness to A was not due to sensory adaptation. Alternatively, detection of A could be tested with other responses that do not habituate. For instance, in a human acoustic-startle response experiment, participants may be asked to raise their hand when they hear the US. Although blinking to the US may decline over repeated presentations, hand raising will likely not, indicating that participants can still hear the US, and thus ruling out the possibility that the decline in blinking was due to sensory adaptation.

Context and non-associative learning. Just as habituation may be confounded with simpler processes such as sensory adaptation and motor fatigue, both sensitization and habituation may be confounded with more complex associative processes. To understand how this may happen, it is important to acknowledge that no stimulus exists in a void. Recall from Chapter 2 that a *stimulus* is an aspect of the environment that may elicit a response. That means that when an aspect of the environment is identified as a stimulus, other aspects of the environment are tacitly identified as *not* that stimulus. Those other aspects of the environment, which may elicit responses of their own, are identified as the *context* of the stimulus. Figure 3.8 is a modification of Figure 2.1 from Chapter

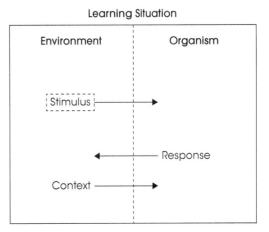

Figure 3.8. Generic representation of a learning situation, incorporating the concept of context; cf., Figure 2.1.

2 that includes the concept of context. The loud sound that serves as US in the acoustic-startle response of the rat is not presented in isolation, but in a particular context, typically a chamber, with readily identifiable features. The head models presented to children in the fixation habituation experiment were not presented in isolation either, but in a laboratory context, which is presumably distinct from other, more typical contexts of an infant, such as his or her home.

Because the US is not presented in isolation but in a context, it is possible that the pairing of US and context, and not simply the repeated presentation of the US, contributes to changes in responsiveness to the US. This confounding effect is particularly prevalent in drug sensitization and tolerance studies. For instance, the sensitizing effect of amphetamine on the locomotion of rats appears to be context-dependent: The locomotion UR to the amphetamine US is substantially stronger if tested in the same context in which it was trained than if tested in a different context (Anagnostaras & Robinson, 1996). Other drug effects become weaker with repeated administration, such as the analgesic effect of morphine (Siegel, 1976). The decline in the efficacy of a drug is known as *drug tolerance* and is a likely contributor to the abuse of certain drugs. On the surface, drug tolerance appears to be an instance of habituation, but several studies in a broad range of drug classes suggest that, like drug sensitization, drug tolerance is context dependent: The UR to a repeatedly-administered drug US is substantially weaker if tested in the same context in which it was trained than if tested in a different context (Siegel, 2005).

There are multiple associative mechanisms that may account for context-dependent changes in behavior; some of them will be reviewed in the next chapters. To isolate the non-associative contribution of repeated stimulation on behavioral change, however, it is important to include the context as a component of the design. This involves, for instance, acknowledging that the presentation of A vs. Not

A during sensitization training (Table 3.2) is really the presentation of A and Context vs. Context alone. Table 3.4 incorporates this acknowledgment, signifying the context with the letter X. If A were tested in context X, it is possible that X, by virtue of being paired with A during training, would contribute to the stronger UR. To rule out that possibility, A may be tested in a different context (Y), and that new context itself should be tested. This alternative test is included in Table 3.4. If the UR to AY is stronger in Experimental subjects than in Control subjects, it must be because of the repeated presentation of A and not because of the pairing of A

CONDITION	TRAINING	SENSITIZATION TEST
Experimental	AX	S: AY / Y
Control	X	R: AY: EXP > CTRL
		Y: EXP = CTRL

Table 3.4. Adjusted design of a sensitization experiment that incorporates context (X). To demonstrate non-associative sensitization, A is tested in a novel context (AY), and the context is tested alone (Y). Stronger response to AY in the experimental condition than in the control condition, but similar response to Y across conditions, would demonstrate a non-associative sensitization of A.

and X. Because it is, in principle, possible that Y contributes to differences in test performance across conditions, Y may be tested alone. Similar response to Y would strengthen the conclusion that A was non-associatively sensitized.

A similar rationale may be applied to the design of a habituation experiment that controls for sensory adaptation and motor fatigue (Table 3.5). If performance on A and B is tested in the same context in which these stimuli were trained (X), it is possible that the stimulus-context pairing (AX and BX), and not just the repeated presentation of each stimulus, contributes to differences in test performance. Testing A and B in a different context (Y), and testing that context alone, may address this potential confound.

CONDITION	TRAINING	HABITUATION TEST
Experimental	AX	S: AY / BY / Y
Control	BX	R: AY: EXP < CTRL
		BY: EXP > CTRL
		Y: EXP = CTRL

Table 3.5. Adjusted design of a habituation experiment. Weaker response to AY in the experimental condition than in the control condition, but similar response to Y across conditions, would demonstrate a non-associative habituation of A.

EXERCISES

Use your example from Box 3.2 to complete the exercises or answer the questions:

1. Draw a (hypothetical) sensitization or habituation graph, tracking the appropriate DV (with units, if appropriate) as a function of the number of presentations of the US (or number of trials). What type of function does your graph show? Use Figure 2.7 in Chapter 2 for reference.

2. Does the demonstration of sensitization or habituation require a control for sensory adaptation or motor fatigue? If so, how would you implement that control?

3. Design a sensitization or habituation test that controls for context-US associations.

4. Design a generalization test for sensitization or habituation. How would you vary the US? Would you vary it during training (as in the Rubel and Rosenthal (1975) chicken study) or during testing (as in the McKenzie et al. (1980) infant study)? Plot some hypothetical results, representing the manipulation of the US in the x-axis and the DV in the y-axis.

REFERENCES

Anagnostaras, S. G., & Robinson, T. E. (1996). Sensitization to the psychomotor stimulant effects of amphetamine: Modulation by associative learning. *Behavioral Neuroscience, 110*(6), 1397–1414.

Aramideh, M., & Ongerboer de Visser, B. W. (2002). Brainstem reflexes: Electrodiagnostic techniques, physiology, normative data, and clinical applications. *Muscle & Nerve, 26*(1), 14–30.

Baerends, G. P., & Kruijt, J. P. (1973). Stimulus selection. In R. A. Hinde & J. Stephenson-Hinde (Eds.), *Constraints on Learning* (pp. 23–50). New York, NY: Academic Press.

Barlow, G. W. (1977). Modal action patterns. In T. A. Sebeok (Ed.), *How animals communicate* (pp. 98–134). Bloomington, IN: Indiana University Press.

Barrett, D. (2010). *Supernormal stimuli: How primal urges overran their evolutionary purpose.* New York, NY: WW Norton & Company.

Cadenhead, K. S., Carasso, B. S., Swerdlow, N. R., Geyer, M. A., & Braff, D. L. (1999). Prepulse inhibition and habituation of the startle response are stable neurobiological measures in a normal male population. *Biological Psychiatry, 45*(3), 360–364.

Cruccu, G., Agostino, R., Berardelli, A., & Manfredi, M. (1986). Excitability of the corneal reflex in man. *Neuroscience Letters, 63*(3), 320–324.

Davis, M. (1974). Sensitization of the rat startle response by noise. *Journal of Comparative and Physiological Psychology, 87*(3), 571–581.

Davis, M. (1989). Sensitization of the acoustic startle reflex by footshock. *Behavioral Neuroscience, 103*(3), 495–503.

De Palo, G., Facchetti, G., Mazzolini, M., Menini, A., Torre, V., & Altafini, C. (2013). Common dynamical features of sensory adaptation in photoreceptors and olfactory sensory neurons. *Scientific Reports, 3*, 1251. doi:10.1038/srep01251

Epstein, L. H., Saad, F. G., Handley, E. A., Roemmich, J. N., Hawk, L. W., & McSweeney, F. K. (2003). Habituation of salivation and motivated responding for food in children. *Appetite, 41*(3), 283–289.

Etcoff, N. L., Stock, S., Haley, L. E., Vickery, S. A., & House, D. M. (2011). Cosmetics as a feature of the extended human phenotype: Modulation of the perception of biologically important facial signals. *PloS one, 6*(10), e25656.

Garland, S. J., & McComas, A. J. (1990). Reflex inhibition of human soleus muscle during fatigue. *The Journal of Physiology, 429*, 17–27.

Ghirlanda, S., & Enquist, M. (2003). A century of generalization. *Animal Behaviour, 66*(1), 15–36.

Grillon, C., Ameli, R., Woods, S. W., Merikangas, K., & Davis, M. (1991). Fear-potentiated startle in humans: Effects of anticipatory anxiety on the acoustic blink reflex. *Psychophysiology, 28*(5), 588–595.

Groves, P. M., & Thompson, R. F. (1970). Habituation: A dual-process theory. *Psychological Review, 77*(5), 419–450.

Heiligenberg, W., & Kramer, U. (1972). Aggressiveness as a function of external stimulation. *Journal of Comparative Physiology A: Neuroethology, Sensory, Neural, and Behavioral Physiology, 77*(3), 332–340.

Heiligenberg, W., Kramer, U., & Schulz, V. (1972). The angular orientation of the black eye-bar in Haplochromis burtoni (Cichlidae, Pisces) and its relevance to aggressivity. *Zeitschrift für vergleichende Physiologie, 76*(2), 168–176.

Itzhak, Y., & Martin, J. L. (1999). Effects of cocaine, nicotine, dizocipline and alcohol on mice locomotor activity: Cocaine–alcohol cross-sensitization involves upregulation of striatal dopamine transporter binding sites. *Brain Research, 818*(2), 204–211.

Khan, O. A., Garcia-Sosa, R., Hageman, J. R., Msall, M., & Kelley, K. R. (2014). Core concepts: Neonatal neurological examination. *NeoReviews, 15*(8), e316–e324.

Kleene, S. J. (2008). The electrochemical basis of odor transduction in vertebrate olfactory cilia. *Chemical Senses, 33*(9), 839–859.

Koch, M., & Schnitzler, H. U. (1997). The acoustic startle response in rats—circuits mediating evocation, inhibition and potentiation. *Behavioural brain research, 89*(1), 35–49.

Lank, D. B., Bousfield, M. A., Cooke, F., & Rockwell, R. F. (1991). Why do snow geese adopt eggs? *Behavioral Ecology, 2*(2), 181–187.

Laughlin, S. B. (1989). The role of sensory adaptation in the retina. *Journal of Experimental Biology, 146*(1), 39–62.

Marshall-Pescini, S., Ceretta, M., & Prato-Previde, E. (2014). Do domestic dogs understand human actions as goal-directed? *PloS one, 9*(9), e106530.

McKenzie, B. E., Tootell, H. E., & Day, R. H. (1980). Development of visual size constancy during the 1st year of human infancy. *Developmental Psychology, 16*(3), 163–174.

Peeke, H. V. S., & Petrinovich, L. (1984). *Habituation, sensitization, and behavior.* Orlando, FL: Academic Press.

Pitman, D. L., Ottenweller, J. E., & Natelson, B. H. (1988). Plasma corticosterone levels during repeated presentation of two intensities of restraint stress: Chronic stress and habituation. *Physiology & Behavior, 43*(1), 47–55.

Rankin, C. H., Abrams, T., Barry, R. J., Bhatnagar, S., Clayton, D. F., Colombo, J., … Marsland, S. (2009). Habituation revisited: An updated and revised description of the behavioral characteristics of habituation. *Neurobiology of Learning and Memory, 92*(2), 135–138.

Rubel, E. W., & Rosenthal, M. H. (1975). The ontogeny of auditory frequency generalization in the chicken. *Journal of Experimental Psychology: Animal Behavior Processes, 1*(4), 287–297.

Siegel, S. (1976). Morphine analgesic tolerance: Its situation specificity supports a Pavlovian conditioning model. *Science, 193*(4250), 323–325.

Siegel, S. (2005). Drug tolerance, drug addiction, and drug anticipation. *Current Directions in Psychological Science, 14*(6), 296–300.

Strakowski, S. M., Sax, K. W., Setters, M. J., & Keck, P. E. (1996). Enhanced response to repeated d-amphetamine challenge: Evidence for behavioral sensitization in humans. *Biological Psychiatry, 40*(9), 872–880.

Thompson, R. F. (2009). Habituation: A history. *Neurobiology of Learning and Memory, 92*(2), 127–134.

Tinbergen, N., & Perdeck, A. C. (1950). On the stimulus situation releasing the begging response in the newly hatched Herring Gull chick (Larus argentatus argentatus Pont.). *Behaviour, 3*, 1–39.

Tinbergen, N., & Van Iersel, J. J. A. (1947). "Displacement reactions" in the three-spined stickleback. *Behaviour, 1*(1), 56–63.

Walker-Andrews, A. S., Krogh-Jespersen, S., Mayhew, E. M., & Coffield, C. N. (2011). Young infants' generalization of emotional expressions: Effects of familiarity. *Emotion, 11*(4), 842–851.

Ware, C. (1980). Coloured illusory triangles due to assimilation. *Perception, 9*(1), 103–107.

Weyer, A. D., Zappia, K. J., Garrison, S. R., O'Hara, C. L., Dodge, A. K., & Stucky, C. L. (2016). Nociceptor sensitization depends on age and pain chronicity. *eneuro, 3*(1). doi:10.1523/ENEURO.0115-15.2015.

Wiley, R. H. (1973). The strut display of male sage grouse: A "fixed" action pattern. *Behaviour, 47*(1), 129–152.

Zafeiriou, D. I. (2004). Primitive reflexes and postural reactions in the neurodevelopmental examination. *Pediatric Neurology, 31*(1), 1–8.

Image Credits

PAVLOVIAN CONDITIONING

4

We have learned so far that behavior may happen—in a healthy animal that is in the appropriate motivational state—solely because of the presentation of a stimulus. We call that stimulus an unconditioned stimulus (US) and the response an unconditioned response (UR). We have also learned about the simplest form of learning, where the magnitude or probability of a UR changes merely because of the repeated presentation of the corresponding US. In this non-associative learning situation, the organism simply learns that a stimulus is being presented repeatedly. If the stimulus is harmless, it is ignored; if the stimulus is harmful, it is attended.

Pavlovian conditioning involves a somewhat more complex form of learning. It is defined as a change in the response to a stimulus caused by the relation of that stimulus to another stimulus. The response that is changed is called a *conditioned response* or CR; the stimulus that elicits the CR is called a *conditioned stimulus* or CS. The stimulus that the CS is related to is a US that elicits a UR, although the nominal US may elicit other responses too.

The historical example of Pavlov's salivating dog provides a good illustration of the concept of Pavlovian conditioning (Figure 1.2 in Chapter 1). In this example, the metronome (CS) acquires the capacity to elicit a salivating response (CR) because it is presented just prior to meat powder (US), which itself elicits salivation (UR). The unconditioned salivation to the meat powder is the kind of behavior described in the preceding chapter; the conditioned salivation to the metronome, although similar in form to meat-elicited salivation, is the kind of Pavlovian-conditioned behavior described in this chapter.

Conditioning, unconditioned behavior, and associative learning. A key feature of Pavlovian conditioning is that, embedded within it, are unconditioned relations between stimuli and responses. The metronome CS is likely to elicit its own unconditioned responses (e.g., orienting), just like the meat powder US unconditionally elicits salivation. Moreover, these unconditioned responses are likely to habituate (or, with stimuli of a different nature, sensitize). What defines Pavlovian conditioning is the change in response that

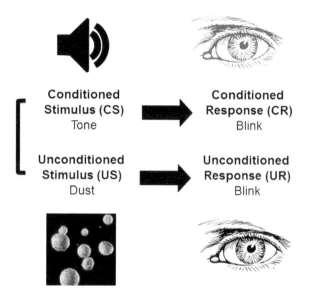

Figure 4.1. Schematic representation of Pavlovian conditioning, with conditioned blinking to a tone as example. The bracket on the left indicates a relation between two stimuli: a tone and dust. Conditioned and unconditioned responses are colored differently to indicate that they can be different.

occurs, not because of the presentation of any particular stimulus, but because of the relation between these stimuli.

Figure 4.1 highlights the role of unconditioned behavior within Pavlovian conditioning (cf. Figure 3.1). Dust in your cornea would elicit blinking without requiring any prior learning. However, if a tone warned you that dust was going to be blown on your eye—maybe the sound of a dust blower revving up—blinking may happen *before* dust hits your eye. Blinking to the tone, unlike blinking to dust, would require a prior learning that the tone precedes dust being blown.

More generally, Pavlovian conditioning demonstrates that the organism has learned an *association* between CS and US—this is why the kind of learning involved in Pavlovian conditioning is called *associative learning*. The salivating dog in Figure 1.2 in Chapter 1 may have learned that the metronome precedes the meat powder; blinking to the tone may indicate that you have learned that the tone precedes blown dust. Associative learning, however, is not necessarily expressed in conditioning performance. Recall from Chapter 1 that performance depends not only on learning, but also on sensorimotor capacity and motivation (Figure 1.1). Even if a dog has learned the association between metronome and meat powder, it may not salivate to the metronome if it is not hungry.

Conditioning and adaptation. Although in the salivation and blinking examples the CR is very similar to the UR, that is not always the case. A rat would normally be startled by a foot shock UR, but it would not be startled by a tone CS that precedes the foot shock; instead, the rat would freeze to that tone. If the CR is often similar to the UR, it is probably because the CS indicates that the US is about to happen, and the most adaptive anticipatory response to the US is often, but not always, similar to the UR. The most adaptive response to imminent food (imagine yourself in a restaurant, waiting for your order) is to salivate; the most adaptive response to imminent dust in your eye is to blink. However, the most adaptive response to foot shock is not a startle response but freezing[1].

The adaptive nature of Pavlovian conditioning is pretty evident: Organisms that learn to anticipate important stimuli may be more effective at exploiting resources, such as food or mates, and avoiding threats, such as predators and natural dangers. This means that Pavlovian conditioning evolved in the context of natural correlations between stimuli: In nature, the best predictor of food (or of a mate or predator) is typically the sight and smell of the food (or of the mate or predator). The taste of rotten food is typically a better predictor of malaise than a 3-kHz tone, or than a red light. Not surprisingly, these natural correlations yield faster and stronger conditioning (Domjan, 2005; Garcia & Koelling, 1966). In the laboratory, however, arbitrary, unnatural, and seemingly neutral stimuli—such as Pavlov's metronome—typically serve as CS. The main reason for such "unnatural" choice is to demonstrate

---

1 Mild foot shock appears to activate defense-behavior systems akin to those of an attack from a predator. If an attack is imminent and escaping is not possible, freezing may reduce the likelihood of being detected and attacked by the predator (Rau & Fanselow, 2007).

more clearly that the change in behavior is due to the pairing of CS and US, avoiding potentially confounding non-associative effects of the CS. The smell of a natural predator, for instance, may unconditionally elicit freezing-like behavior (Dielenberg & McGregor, 2001), even though it may also acquire CS properties, perhaps more readily than a tone or light. To demonstrate Pavlovian conditioning, such confound effects must be controlled for. Thus, researchers often exploit the versatility of Pavlovian conditioning to study the mechanisms that govern it.

DEMONSTRATING PAVLOVIAN CONDITIONING

Pavlovian contingency. Pavlovian conditioning is defined in terms of the relation between stimuli. The term *relation* in this context is somewhat ambiguous—and intentionally so. It connotes a kind of regularity or correlation between the related stimuli. More often than not, such regularity is temporal in nature as the CS *precedes* the US in time. A tone that is presented simultaneously with dust is not an effective warning signal and is unlikely to elicit a blinking CR. It is also important to note that the temporal ordering between CS and US is not as important as the correlation between the two stimuli. A tone CS that is always present, strictly speaking, precedes the dust US, but it also follows the dust US and is present simultaneously with the dust US—thus it is not a very useful warning signal, and such tone would not be related to the dust stimulus in a Pavlovian sense. The absence of the US in the absence of the CS is just as important in establishing a relation between these stimuli as the presence of the US in the presence of the CS (Rescorla, 1967b).

More technically, the relation between CS and US is expressed in terms of the *contingency* between CS and US. Figure 4.2 illustrates the notion of contingency between stimuli. Contingency between CS and US is a continuous variable that ranges between very positive to very negative. Contingency between the CS and US is positive if the probability of the US given the CS, p(US|CS), is higher than the probability of the US given the absence of the CS, p(US|~CS) (top-left of the plot in Figure 4.2). Contingency between the CS and US is negative if p(US|CS) is lower than p(US|~CS) (bottom-right of the plot in Figure 4.2; Rescola, 1967b). In both cases the CS is informative of the US: With positive contingency the CS indicates the presence of the US; with negative contingency the CS indicates the absence of the US. As p(US|CS) becomes more similar to p(US|~CS), the CS becomes less informative of the US; when p(US|CS) = p(US|~CS) (diagonal line in Figure 4.2), the CS is not informative of the US, and the US is said to be non-contingent to the CS.

Positive and negative contingencies are common in nature and in daily life. For instance, the contingency between dark clouds and rain is very positive:

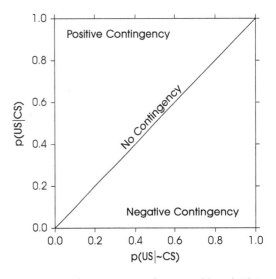

Figure 4.2. The contingency between CS and US is defined as the difference between the probability of the US given the CS, p(US|CS) in the y-axis, and the probability of the US given no CS, p(US|~CS) in the x-axis. Positive differences (top-left corner of plot) constitute positive contingencies; negative differences (bottom-right corner of plot) constitute negative contingences. When p(US|CS) = p(US|~CS) (diagonal line), there is no contingency between CS and US.

The probability of rain with dark clouds is higher than the probability of rain with a clear sky. The contingency between dark clouds and sunburn, on the other hand, is very negative: the probability of sunburn with dark clouds is lower than the probability of sunburn when clouds are absent. In the box, write down two examples, one of a positive contingency and one of a negative contingency, both drawn from your own experience. Identify the two stimuli involved in each contingency, identified as *earlier* and *later*, where the earlier stimulus precedes the later stimulus when they are contingent (just like a CS normally precedes a US, and dark clouds precede the absence of sunburn). In the positive contingency example, how would you respond to earlier stimulus? (You can get some ideas from Exercise 1 in this chapter, but do not copy those examples.)

Box 4.1

_____

Positive Contingency

Earlier Stimulus: Later Stimulus:

Response to Earlier Stimulus:

Negative Contingency

Earlier Stimulus: Later Stimulus:

_____

Notice that most examples of Pavlovian conditioning so far involve positive contingencies, that is, CSs are informative of the presence of USs (e.g., a metronome indicating that food will be delivered). This particular form of conditioning is called *excitatory Pavlovian conditioning*. Conditioning that involves negative contingencies is called *inhibitory Pavlovian conditioning*. In this form of conditioning, the organism learns that the CS indicates the absence of the US. In terms of its adaptive value, inhibitory Pavlovian learning is just as important as excitatory Pavlovian learning. Learning when predators or food are absent, for instance, may result in more efficient foraging behavior. Demonstrating inhibitory conditioning in the laboratory, however, is substantially more difficult than demonstrating excitatory conditioning. A rat that has learned that a tone is never followed by foot shock behaves very similarly to a rat that has not learned that relation. The techniques and control conditions involved in the demonstration of inhibitory conditioning are complex enough to merit a separate discussion. The remainder of this chapter will thus focus mostly on excitatory conditioning, keeping in mind that this form of conditioning represents only one side of the Pavlovian learning "coin." Interested readers are referred to key literature (Christianson et al., 2012; Miller & Spear, 1985; Rescorla, 1969; Savastano, Cole, Barnet, & Miller, 1999; Williams, Overmier, & LoLordo, 1992).

If the contingency between CS and US, positive or negative, defines Pavlovian conditioning, then how strong should such contingency be for these stimuli to be related in a Pavlovian sense? That is, how different should p(US|CS) and p(US|~CS) be? The continuous nature of this difference precludes singling out any particular level of contingency above which two stimuli are considered related, and below which they are considered not related. Instead, by definition, the function that relates contingency and conditioning strength is expected to be monotonic with a positive slope (see Figure 2.7 in Chapter 2): A more positive contingency should yield a stronger (or more probable) CR, all else being equal. If broad changes in contingency do not change the ostensive CR, then that response cannot be attributed to Pavlovian conditioning.

Control conditions. The notion of contingency provides the rationale for two typical control conditions for the demonstration of excitatory Pavlovian conditioning: the random control condition and the explicitly unpaired condition (Rescorla, 1967b). These conditions are illustrated in Figure 4.3. The random control condition involves presenting CS and US independently and at random times. The explicitly unpaired condition involves presenting the CS without the US, and the US without the CS; this condition imposes

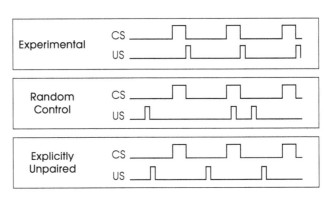

Figure 4.3. Experimental and control conditions for Pavlovian conditioning. The upticks and downticks in the timelines indicate the moments when the CS and US are turned on and off, respectively.

a negative contingency between CS and US. To the extent that the positive CS-US contingency is sufficient and necessary to elicit a CR, the CR should not appear in either control condition.

The random control and explicitly unpaired conditions rule out the possibility that the nominal CS alone elicits the CR. Of course, it would be highly likely that something other than Pavlovian conditioning is taking place if the first presentation of the CS elicited the CR (e.g., if Pavlov's dog salivated to the first presentation of the metronome). But such a confound is not always that evident. Consider the situation where the CS alone elicits a weak CR, which gets stronger over multiple presentations of the CS (i.e., where the CR sensitizes). This is unlikely the case with sounds that elicit salivation, but it is more likely when the CS is a stimulant drug (e.g., Besheer, Palmatier, Metschke, & Bevins, 2004). If the CR is a locomotor response, such as nosing the location where an appetitive US is expected, such response may sensitize over the repeated presentation of a stimulant CS. It would be easy (and incorrect) to infer that the organism has learned the association between stimulant CS and appetitive US, when in reality no such association may have formed.

Table 4.1 shows the design of an excitatory Pavlovian conditioning experiment. The Experimental and Control conditions are very similar, except that the US is positively contingent to the CS (A) in the Experimental condition, but not in the Control condition. In the Control condition, the US is

CONDITION	TRAINING	TEST
Experimental	A+	S: A
Control	A−	R: EXP > CTRL

Table 4.1. Design of an excitatory Pavlovian conditioning experiment. The letter A signifies a conditioned stimulus (CS), either paired with the US (+) or not (–). A stronger conditioned response (CR) to A in the Experimental condition than in the Control condition would demonstrate Pavlovian conditioning of A in the Experimental group.

either non-contingent or negatively contingent to A—either case is typically represented with a minus ("–") sign following the label for the CS.

The experimental design described in Table 4.1 corresponds to a *between-subject* design of Pavlovian conditioning, where the same stimulus A is presented to two groups of subjects under different training conditions. Alternatively, these experimental conditions may be implemented in a *within-subject* design. This implementation requires two CSs, A and B, one experimental (A+), and one control (B–); A would be presented just prior to the US, whereas B would be presented either randomly or in an explicitly unpaired way. A stronger CR to A than to B would demonstrate Pavlovian conditioning of A. It is important to highlight that the specific stimulus represented by A and B are typically counterbalanced among subjects. For instance, for half of the subjects A could be a light and B a tone, whereas for the other half A could be a tone and B a light. Such counterbalanced arrangement prevents confounding *stimulus effects* (e.g., the light may be more likely to elicit the nominal CR unconditionally) with conditioning effects.

THE TEMPORAL ARRANGEMENT OF CS AND US

Figure 4.4 describes five ways in which CS and US may be arranged over time. The most common arrangement is called *short-delay* conditioning. In this arrangement, the *CS–US interval* (the time between CS onset and US onset) is short, and the offset of the CS is simultaneous to, or happens shortly after, the onset of the US. This is a particularly effective way of training the CS to elicit an anticipatory response to the US. If the CS is short enough, the CR may be elicited very shortly after the onset of the CS. The interval between CS onset and CR, called the *CR latency*, may not be shorter than the time it takes to detect the CS and execute the CR.

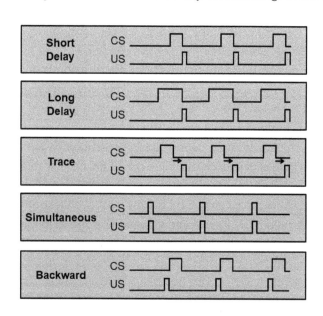

Another form of delayed conditioning involves a relatively long CS-US interval called *long-delay* conditioning. In this preparation, the CR latency is substantially longer than its minimum. In fact, the onset of the CS may suppress the spontaneous production of the CR, an effect known as *inhibition of delay* (Rescorla, 1967a). Long CR latencies and inhibition of delay suggest that the timing of the CR tracks the timing of the US (Drew, Zupan, Cooke, Couvillon, & Balsam, 2005). This hypothesis suggests that organisms may respond to the temporal proximity of the US, as signaled by the passage of time in the presence of the CS. Whereas in short-delay conditioning

Figure 4.4. Variations in the temporal arrangement of CS and US in Pavlovian conditioning. The upticks and downticks in the timelines indicate the moments when the CS and US are turned on and off, respectively. In trace conditioning, each trace interval is marked with an arrow.

the onset of the CS signals the temporal proximity of the US, in long-term conditioning it signals the temporal remoteness of the US. Note that typical CRs are those that are appropriate to proximal USs (you are unlikely to blink for dust that will be blown in a few minutes). Therefore, the onset of a long-delay CS may elicit the appropriate response to a US that will not happen soon (Silva & Timberlake, 1998).

Unlike short- and long-delay conditioning, in *trace* conditioning the interval between CS offset and US onset, known as the *trace interval*, is greater than zero (see arrows in Figure 4.4). To appreciate the significance of this seemingly minor parametric change in the arrangement of stimuli, consider what the organism experiences on a moment-by-moment basis. Between the last US and the subsequent CS, the organism experiences the absence of both CS and US. The interval between these stimuli is called the *inter-trial interval* or ITI (the presentation of CS and US is often referred to as a *trial*). Just as during the ITI, the organism experiences the absence of both CS and US during the trace interval. However, whereas the ITI is temporally removed from the US, the trace interval is temporally adjacent to the US. Thus, in trace conditioning, very similar stimuli (or, rather, the absence thereof) are related in opposite ways to the US. It is thus not surprising that, relative to delay conditioning, trace conditioning is acquired more slowly and recruits neural mechanisms involved in memory and cognition (Solomon, Vander Schaaf, Thompson, & Weisz, 1986).

The last two forms of conditioning are less likely to yield, on their own, robust CRs. *Simultaneous conditioning* involves the concurrent presentation of CS and US; *backward conditioning* involves the presentation of the US prior to the CS. To the extent that the CR expresses an anticipation of the US, neither a simultaneous nor a backward CS and US is likely to elicit a CR. The absence of a CR, however, does not mean the absence of learning. If, as suggested with long-delayed conditioning, the organism learns the temporal arrangement between CS and US, it is possible for the organism to learn that the CS happens at the same time or even following the US. Of course, the demonstration of such learning cannot be based on an anticipatory CR. Instead, such demonstration requires more sophisticated and indirect methods that are beyond the scope of this chapter (Savastano & Miller, 1998).

EXPERIMENTAL PARADIGMS

Pavlovian conditioning is typically studied in small laboratory animals, such as rodents and small birds, but a wide variety of other species—from invertebrates (e.g., Daly & Smith, 2000) to human and non-human primates—have also served as subjects. The prevalent use of rodents and birds assumes that the principles that govern Pavlovian conditioning are phenotypes that are well preserved across species, at least across vertebrates. These animals are also relatively easy to house in large numbers, and thus afford the level of control that is required for experimental research. Training and testing can be conducted in small, automated environments. Small animals also provide direct access to brains for examination, which may unveil the neurobiological substrate of Pavlovian conditioning.

Implementations of Pavlovian conditioning may be grouped in at least two categories, according to the nature of the US: those that use an appetitive US (e.g., food, mate) and those that use an aversive US (e.g., electric shock, unpleasant flavors). Appetitive stimuli elicit unconditional approach responses (*adience*), whereas aversive stimuli elicit unconditional repulsion (*abience*).

Appetitive paradigms. The most simple appetitive Pavlovian paradigm is the *Pavlovian conditioned approach* procedure. In this paradigm, an arbitrary CS (e.g., a light, a tone) precedes the delivery of an appetitive US (food, access to a mate). If the CS is relatively diffuse (e.g., ambient light, or an tone that is audible from a distance), it often elicits an approach response to the location of the US (Holland, 1977, 1980), although it may also elicit other behaviors such as undirected locomotion. The conditioned approach to the location of the US, called *goal tracking*, is relatively intuitive: If a cue indicates impending food to a hungry organism, it makes sense that the cue will elicit an approach response to the location of food. Such behavior, to the extent that it is elicited more than under control conditions, serves as evidence that the organism has learned the cue-food association.

A localized CS (e.g., a small light, the extension of a lever) that signals an appetitive US, on the other hand, often elicits an approach response to the location of the CS, not of the US (Brown & Jenkins, 1968; Domjan, Lyons, North, & Bruell, 1986; Hearst & Jenkins, 1974; Holland, 1980). The conditioned approach to the location of the CS, called *sign tracking* or *autoshaping*, is less intuitive than goal tracking. In birds, sign tracking is typically trained by illuminating a key (a button similar to those in elevators) once in a while and for a few seconds, just before delivering food; sign tracking is expressed as pecks on the key. In rodents, sign tracking is typically trained by occasionally extending a lever for a few seconds, just before delivering food; sign tracking is expressed as lever presses.

Why would an organism approach the location of the CS instead of the location of an appetitive US, even when such behavior reduces contact with the appetitive US (Hearst & Jenkins, 1974; Van Hest, Van Haaren, Kop, & Van der Schoot, 1986)? An evolutionary account suggests that because in natural environments CS and US are typically in the same place (food is located where it is sighted; a mate is located where it is heard), approaching the CS normally maximizes the likelihood of contacting the US. A more proximal mechanism that governs sign tracking may be the acquisition of rewarding properties—or *incentive salience*—by the CS (Uslaner, Acerbo, Jones, & Robinson, 2006). According to this hypothesis, the CS not only becomes informative of the impending appetitive US (as in the case of goal tracking), but it also acquires the properties of an appetitive stimulus itself, which elicits approach. The capacity of localized CSs to elicit sign tracking—and, presumably, to acquire incentive salience—varies substantially between individual organisms and may be associated with vulnerability to substance dependence (Flagel, Akil, & Robinson, 2009).

Sign tracking is a practical method to assess the rewarding properties of a stimulus. However, the rewarding properties of drugs are more often evaluated in rodents through the approach to and dwelling in drug-associated contexts. In the *conditioned place preference* (CPP) paradigm (Tzschentke, 2007), a small enclosure is divided by a door into two spaces, each with distinct visual and olfactory properties. In a common variation of CPP, baseline preference for each of the two spaces is determined by opening the dividing door, allowing the subject to move between spaces. The space where the subject spends less time is identified as the non-preferred side. In training trials, the dividing door is closed and subjects are confined alternately and for short periods of time (typically 10 to 30 minutes, once or twice per day) in their non-preferred and preferred side. Before each placement on the non-preferred side, subjects are injected with the drug under evaluation that is diluted in a vehicle solution, so that the psychotropic effects of the drug are experienced in the non-preferred side. Right before each placement on the preferred side, subjects are injected just with the vehicle solution, which has no psychotropic effects. Through this alternated placement, the non-preferred side may be trained as a CS for the psychotropic US, which elicits approach and indwelling. This CR is assessed in a choice test, identical to baseline preference assessment: The subject is placed in the CPP apparatus with the dividing door open, and time spent on each space is measured. Spending more time in the originally non-preferred side during the choice test is indicative of that space becoming a CS for an appetitive drug US.

Aversive paradigms. Aversive Pavlovian paradigms include conditioned eyeblink, fear conditioning, and taste aversion. Conditioned eyeblink is typically implemented in rabbits (Gormezano, Schneiderman, Deaux, & Fuentes, 1962) and, less often, in humans (Sears, Finn, & Steinmetz, 1994). It involves the presentation of an arbitrary CS shortly before blowing a puff of air on the eye of an organism. In rabbits, the CS elicits a brief movement of the nictitating membrane, akin to the closure of the eyelid.

In fear conditioning, an arbitrary CS is presented before inescapable electric shock is delivered (Maren, 2001). In rodents, shock is typically delivered to the foot through the floor in a chamber. The CR of rodents to a fearful CS is *freezing*—the absence of movement, except for breathing. Although freezing is often times measured on the basis of video recordings of the animal's activity, an alternative technique consists of measuring the disruption of another behavior. For instance, a rat may be trained first to press a lever for food (see Chapter 5); because freezing is inconsistent with lever pressing, fear conditioning may be evident as a CS-induced decline in lever pressing (Bouton & Bolles, 1980; Estes & Skinner, 1941). This technique, called *conditioned suppression*, is particularly practical, because it permits an automated quantification of the CR through the difference between pressing the lever in the presence of the CS and in its absence. The typical dependent measure of conditioned suppression is the *suppression ratio*. To measure the suppression ratio, the number of lever presses is counted during the fear-eliciting CS (B_T) and during an identical interval just prior to the CS (B_I). The suppression ratio is $B_T / (B_T + B_I)$; lower suppression ratios—particularly those lower than 0.5—are indicative of fear conditioning. It is important to highlight that even though a fearful CS suppresses food-reinforced lever pressing, such CS is excitatory, not inhibitory, because it predicts the presence of the US.

Conditioned taste aversion involves the presentation of a flavor CS, typically delivered in water, mixed with a nausea-inducing chemical, such as lithium chloride (Welzl, D'Adamo, & Lipp, 2001). The CR to the flavor CS is a rejection of the flavor, expressed as reduced consumption and, if consumption is forced, orofacial expressions related to disgust.

LEARNING MECHANISMS

Pavlovian conditioning involves, by definition, a contingency between CS and US; control conditions involve breaking or at least changing such contingency. Such a definitional role of contingency, however, does not specify the nature of the learned CS-US association or the mechanism through which it is learned. It is possible, for instance, that in Pavlovian conditioning organisms learn the difference between p(US|CS) and p(US|~CS). A more parsimonious alternative, however, suggests that mere contiguity between CS and US is sufficient to explain Pavlovian conditioning (Papini & Bitterman, 1990). In such a case, instead of learning the differences between probabilities, the organism would only be required to have a relatively short memory of the CS while the US is present—Wagner (2008) provides an insightful elaboration on this idea. The contiguity hypothesis would explain, for instance, why delayed conditioning is more robust than trace conditioning (Weike, Schupp, & Hamm, 2007).

Overshadowing and blocking. Despite the parsimony of a simple contiguity mechanism underlying Pavlovian conditioning, several well-established experimental findings undermine this hypothesis. The first such finding is an effect called *overshadowing* (Kamin, 1969). Table 4.2 shows the experimental design for the demonstration of overshadowing.

CONDITION	TRAINING	TEST
Experimental	AB+	S: A / B
Control	A+ / B+	R: EXP < CTRL

Table 4.2. Experimental design for the demonstration of overshadowing. The letters A and B signify conditioned stimuli (CSs). The plus (+) sign indicates when a CS is followed by the US. The slash (/) indicates when stimuli are presented separately. Conditioned responding (CR) to A and B, presented separately, is weaker when A and B are trained together (Experimental condition) than when A and B are trained separately (Control condition).

CONDITION	TRAINING (PHASE 1)	TRAINING (PHASE 2)	TEST
Experimental	A+	AC+	S: C
Control	B+		R: EXP < CTRL

Table 4.3. Experimental design for the demonstration of blocking. When C is trained with a previously experienced stimulus A (Experimental group), CR to C is weaker than when C is trained with a novel stimulus (Control group).

Experimental subjects are trained with two simultaneous CSs, labeled A and B (this is called a *compound* CS); control subjects are trained with the same stimuli presented separately. If conditioning depends solely on the contiguity between CS and US, no difference between experimental and control subjects should be observed in CR to A and B during the test, because A and B are equally contiguous to the US during training. CR is typically weaker, however, when A and B are trained simultaneously rather than separately.

Another effect that undermines the contiguity hypothesis is called *blocking* (Arcediano, Matute, & Miller, 1997; Kamin, 1969). Table 4.3 shows the experimental design for the demonstration of blocking. Experimental and control subjects are first trained with different CSs (Phase 1), and then with the same compound CS (Phase 2). The compound CS includes a CS that is novel to all subjects (C), and a stimulus that is novel only to control subjects (A). If conditioning depends solely on the contiguity between CS and US, no difference between experimental and control subjects should be observed in CR to C during the test because C is equally contiguous to the US during training. CR is typically weaker, however, when C is trained along with an experienced CS rather than with a novel CS.

In overshadowing and blocking, subjects that are equally exposed to a contiguous CS-US pair respond differently to the CS because of their training with another CS. These effects rule out the possibility that simple contiguity between CS and US can explain Pavlovian conditioning. It does not rule out, however, more complex contiguity-based accounts of Pavlovian learning. One such account—which explains overshadowing and blocking—is the Rescorla-Wagner model (Rescorla & Wagner, 1972).

The Rescorla-Wagner Model

The Rescorla-Wagner model is fairly simple. It is important to keep in mind, however, that it is not a model of conditioned responding, but a model of learning. That is, it predicts a variable that is not directly observable: the change in *associative strength* between CS and US, represented as ΔV. Aside from being hypothetical, the associative strength of a CS is also unit-less. The model assumes, however, that ΔV is positively related to the magnitude and probability of the CR (Figure 2.7 in Chapter 2, Panels A and C). Therefore, the model predicts whether CR should increase, decrease, or remain unchanged, but—despite being a mathematical model—it cannot predict by how much.

The simplest mathematical expression of the Rescorla-Wagner model is

$$\Delta V_x = k(\lambda - V_T). \tag{6.1}$$

ΔV_x is the change in associative strength between CS X and a US after a trial in which X was present. That is, after trial n, $\Delta V_x = V_{X,n} - V_{X,n-1}$, where $V_{X,n}$ is the associative strength of CS X immediately *after* trial n, and $V_{X,n-1}$ is the associative strength of CS X immediately *before* trial n. V_T is the sum of the associative strengths of *all* CSs present in that trial, including X. That is, $V_T = V_{A,n-1} + V_{B,n-1} + V_{C,n-1} + ...$ $V_{X,n-1}$, where CSs A, B, C, X, etc. were present in trial n. λ is the maximum associative strength that the US present on a given trial can support. This implies that, when the US is absent in a trial, $\lambda = 0$ for that trial. k is the rate of learning, which is relatively constant and depends on characteristics of the CS and the US. k ranges between zero (no learning) and 1 (instantaneous learning).

Excitatory conditioning. To illustrate the implications of the Rescorla-Wagner model, consider first a relatively simple situation: A single CS is repeatedly presented with the US on every trial. Assume that, prior to the first trial ($n = 0$), the CS has no associative strength, so $V_{X,0} = V_T = 0$. Assume also that $\lambda = 100$ and $k = .10$. In the first trial, the difference between λ and V_T is therefore 100. Equation 6.1 indicates that the associative strength of the CS increases by 10 percent of that difference, which is .10 × 100 = 10. Therefore, $V_{X,1} = 10$. In the second trial, V_T is updated to 10 (remember, there is only one CS, so the associative strength of that CS is also V_T). The difference between λ and V_T is therefore smaller than in the previous trial: 90 instead of 100. After the second trial, the associative strength of the CS increases again by 10 percent of that difference, which is 9, so it increases from 10 to 19. If you repeat this sequence, you will find that V_X on trials $n = 3$, 4, 5, 6, etc. is 27.10, 34.39, 40.95, 46.86, etc. Note that V_X increases in smaller steps (10 on $n = 1$, 9 on $n = 2$, 8.1 on $n = 3$, etc.) Those steps are represented as ΔV_X, which becomes smaller with repeated training. In fact, with sufficient training, ΔV_X will be virtually zero, which is when V_X is almost equal to λ, and therefore $\lambda - V_T$ is approximately zero. If you trace V_X as a function of trial in this example, you will see that V_X is a negatively accelerated function of trial with a positive slope (Figure 4.5, left portion of the graph).

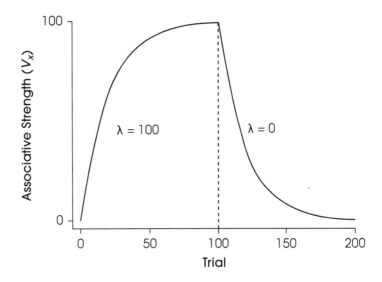

Figure 4.5. Simulation of the Rescorla-Wagner model (Equation 6.1), tracing the associative strength of CS X to a US (V_X) as a function of training trials. In the first 100 trials (left portion of the graph), the US is present on every trial ($\lambda = 100$). In the last 100 trials (right portion of the graph), the US is absent on every trial ($\lambda = 0$). k is set to .05 throughout.

The previous example illustrates a key feature of the Rescorla-Wagner model. If you think of the CS as setting an expectation about the US, Pavlovian learning happens when such expectation is violated (i.e., when the US is "surprising"). Learning consists, from this perspective, on lining up expectations (elicited by the CS) with outcomes (the US). Initially, Pavlov's dog does not expect a food US when the metronome CS is presented (i.e., $V_{metronome,0} = V_T = 0$). With repeated presentations of the metronome, its associative strength increases until the dog learns to expect the food US when the metronome is present ($V_T = \lambda$, and therefore $\Delta V_X = 0$).

The Rescorla-Wagner model explains not only the acquisition of a CR, but also its *extinction*. Extinction refers to the decline of an acquired CR due to the discontinuation of the US. Note that removal of the US implies a removal of the CS-US contingency, p(US|CS) = p(US|~CS) = 0, so, to the extent that a response is a Pavlovian CR, extinction implies a reduction in the CR. In the Rescorla-Wagner model, extinction is instantiated by setting $\lambda = 0$ (the absence of the US maintains no associative strength) with $V_{X,0} = V_T > \lambda$. As in the acquisition example, repeated trials result in the progressive approximation of V_X to λ, with ΔV_X approaching zero (Figure 4.5, right portion of the graph). The subject starts with an expectation of the US, but the expectation progressively declines as it is repeatedly violated.

The acquisition and extinction of a CR involve only excitatory conditioning, which in the Rescorla-Wagner model is expressed as *positive* associative strength (i.e., $V_X > 0$). This model also explains inhibitory conditioning, expressing it as *negative* associative strength (i.e., $V_X < 0$). To illustrate how a CS may acquire negative associative strength, we must consider (a) the role of context in Pavlovian conditioning, and (b) how the Rescorla-Wagner model treats compound stimuli.

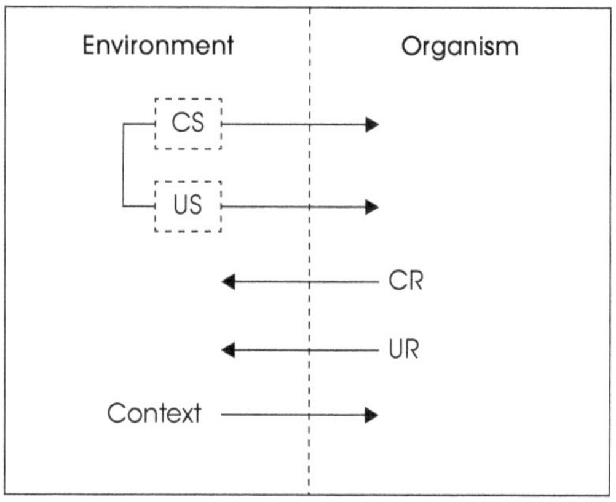

Inhibitory conditioning. Recall our discussion on the role of context in non-associative learning. Just as habituated and sensitized stimuli are not presented in a void, CSs and USs are not presented in a void either (Figure 4.6). It is evident, therefore, that the absence of the CS in the ITI is more accurately described as the presence of the context alone, and that the presence of the CS during a trial is more accurately described as the presence of a compound stimulus: the CS and the context. When the CS and the US are explicitly unpaired (negative contingency), the US is present only with the context, and it is absent when the CS and context are present. Therefore, the Rescorla-Wagner model treats the context as another CS and, in explicitly unpaired training, $V_T = V_{context}$ when $\lambda > 0$, and $V_T = V_{context} + V_{CS}$ when $\lambda = 0$. Using the parameters from the acquisition example ($V_{context,0} = V_{CS,0} = 0$, $k = .10$, $\lambda = 100$ when US is present), Table 4.4 shows how, under a negative contingency, the CS becomes a conditioned inhibitor (V_{CS} becomes negative) according to the Rescorla-Wagner model.

Figure 4.6. Representation of a Pavlovian learning situation, incorporating the concept of context.

Just as during Pavlovian acquisition and extinction, during negative contingency training V_T progressively approaches λ (100), increasing over the course of 10 ITIs from zero to 42.65. This happens because $V_{context}$ becomes increasingly positive over training. $V_{context}$ also drives V_T upward when the CS is present, but the increase in V_T is decelerated and, between trials 9 and 10, V_T begins to decline. This late push downwards happens because V_{CS} becomes increasingly negative over training. With sufficient training, the subject learns to expect the US during the ITI ($V_T = V_{context} = 100 = \lambda$) and not when the CS is present ($V_T = V_{context} + V_{CS} = 100 - 100 = 0 = \lambda$).

Accounting for blocking and overshadowing. The Rescorla-Wagner model can explain the acquisition and extinction of excitatory and inhibitory learning, all on the basis of the contiguity of CS and US. This model does not require subjects to learn the positive or negative correlation between CS

TRIAL	CS PRESENT?	V_T	λ	$\Delta V_{context}$	$V_{context}$	ΔV_{CS}	V_{CS}
1	Yes	0.00	0	0.00	0.00	0.00	0.00
ITI	No	0.00	100	10.00	10.00	0.00	0.00
2	Yes	10.00	0	−1.00	9.00	−1.00	−1.00
ITI	No	9.00	100	9.10	18.10	0.00	−1.00
3	Yes	17.10	0	−1.71	16.39	−1.71	−2.71
ITI	No	16.39	100	8.36	24.75	0.00	−2.71
4	Yes	22.04	0	−2.20	22.55	−2.20	−4.91
ITI	No	22.55	100	7.74	30.29	0.00	−4.91
5	Yes	25.38	0	−2.54	27.75	−2.54	−7.45
ITI	No	27.75	100	7.23	34.98	0.00	−7.45
6	Yes	27.53	0	−2.75	32.23	−2.75	−10.20
ITI	No	32.23	100	6.77	39.00	0.00	−10.20
7	Yes	28.80	0	−2.88	36.12	−2.88	−13.08
ITI	No	36.12	100	6.39	42.51	0.00	−13.08
8	Yes	29.43	0	−2.94	39.57	−2.95	−16.03
ITI	No	39.57	100	6.04	45.61	0.00	−16.03
9	Yes	29.58	0	−2.96	42.65	−2.96	−18.99
ITI	No	42.65	100	5.74	48.39	0.00	−18.99
10	Yes	29.40	0	−2.94	45.45	−2.94	−21.93

Table 4.4. An example of Rescorla-Wagner model parameters varying during Pavlovian inhibitory training. The example assumes $V_{context,0} = V_{CS,0} = 0$, $k = .10$, and, when the CS is present, $\lambda = 0$.

and US. Instead, it explains how the expectation of the presence or absence of the US may emerge from a contiguity mechanism.

The Rescorla-Wagner model can also explain the two effects that ruled out a simple contiguity mechanism of Pavlovian learning, overshadowing and blocking. The rationale is fairly simple: In the case of overshadowing, the associative strength derived from the US must be divided between the two CSs, making each less likely of eliciting a strong CR than if they had been trained in isolation. With sufficient training, experimental subjects in Table 4.2 would expect λ from CSs A and B *together*, which means that $V_A + V_B = \lambda$, which, in turn, means that V_A and V_B are each likely to be lower than λ. With the same training, control subjects in Table 4.2 would expect λ from CSs A and B *separately*, which means that $V_A = V_B = \lambda$. Put in plain English, whereas experimental subjects must divide the "credit" for the US between A and B, control subjects do not. Therefore, experimental subjects are expected to respond less to A and B than control subjects.

In the case of blocking, at the end of training phase 1, $V_A = \lambda$ for experimental subjects, but $V_A = 0$ for control subjects. At the beginning of training phase 2, $V_C = 0$ for both groups. Therefore, for experimental subjects early in phase 2, $V_T = V_A + V_C = \lambda + 0 = \lambda$, so $\Delta V_A = \Delta V_C = k(\lambda - V_T) = k \times 0 = 0$, and no learning occurs. In contrast, for control subjects early in phase 2, $V_T = V_A + V_C = 0 + 0 = 0$, so $\Delta V_A = \Delta V_C = k(\lambda - V_T) = k\lambda$, and learning does occur at rate k. Put in plain English, whereas experimental subjects prior to phase 2 have assigned all credit for the US to A, control subjects have not. Therefore, experimental subjects are expected to respond less to C than control subjects.

Generalization. Just like habituated and sensitized stimuli, Pavlovian CSs generalize: The more different the test stimulus is to the trained CS, the weaker the observed CR (e.g., Lissek et al., 2008). After training a metronome-food association, it is likely that sounds similar to those of a metronome would elicit a weaker salivation CR than the trained metronome CS. The Rescorla-Wagner model provides a framework to understand Pavlovian generalization (Pearce, 1987). A CS (A) may be thought of as a compound stimulus comprising multiple elementary stimuli (A1, A2, A3, …, An). According to the Rescorla-Wagner model, after sufficient training, $V_{A1} + V_{A2} + V_{A3} + \ldots + V_{An} = \lambda$. That is, the associative strength of A is distributed among its elements. Changing A just slightly—like changing the metronome for a similar sound—would be equivalent to substituting a few elements of A for new elements that have no associative strength. Because the associative strength of a compound stimulus is the sum of the associative strength of its elements, this substitution entails a reduction in the associative strength of the new compound stimulus relative to the old compound stimulus: If V_{A1} were substituted with $V_{B1} = 0$, then $V_{B1} + V_{A2} + V_{A3} + \ldots + V_{An} < \lambda$. The associative strength of the new compound stimulus declines as more elements are changed, yielding a generalization gradient.

CONDITION	TRAINING (PHASE 1)	TRAINING (PHASE 2)	TEST
Experimental	C+	CA+	S: CA
Control	C−		R: EXP < CTRL

Table 4.5. Experimental design for the demonstration of the US pre-exposure effect. When A is trained with a US previously experienced in the same context (Experimental group), CR to A is weaker than when A is trained with a novel US (Control group).

US pre-exposure and latent inhibition. The Rescorla-Wagner model explains other interesting effects, including the reduced efficacy of a previously presented US. The design of the US pre-exposure demonstration is shown in Table 4.5. Experimental subjects are first trained with exposure to context C along with the US, whereas control subjects are exposed to context C alone. Then, both groups are trained with CS A in context C. When A is tested in context C, experimental subjects display a weaker CR than control subjects. The cause of this difference, according to the Rescorla-Wagner model, is fairly straightforward: Context C blocks the conditioning of A for experimental subjects but not for control subjects. Although context C is strongly conditioned in experimental subjects, the expression of the corresponding CR is weak because of the diffuse nature of the context (in particular in the case of sign tracking).

CONDITION	TRAINING (PHASE 1)	TRAINING (PHASE 2)	TEST
Experimental	A−	A+	S: A
Control	B−		R: EXP < CTRL

Table 4.6. Experimental design for the demonstration of the latent inhibition. When A is trained after being presented without the US (Experimental group), CR to A is weaker than when A is novel (Control group).

Just like US pre-exposure yields weaker conditioning, so does CS pre-exposure. The latter effect is called *latent inhibition*. Unlike US pre-exposure, however, latent inhibition has garnered a substantial amount of attention because of its relation to schizophrenia: Individuals suffering from this mental disorder are less likely to display latent inhibition (Lubow & Gewirtz, 1995; Lubow & Weiner, 2010). Also unlike US pre-exposure, the Rescorla-Wagner model cannot account for latent inhibition (Miller, Barnet & Grahame, 1995). To understand this, consider the experimental design for the demonstration of latent inhibition, shown in Table 4.6. The Rescorla-Wagner model predicts that nothing should be learned in training phase 1 about a CS with no associative strength ($V_T = V_A = 0$) in the absence of the

POST-EXTINCTION EFFECT	CAUSE OF RECOVERY OF EXTINGUISHED CS
Spontaneous recovery	Prolonged period without exposure to the CS or the extinction context (Rescorla, 2004).
Renewal	Change in the context of extinction (Bouton & King, 1983).
Reinstatement	Presentation of the US without the CS (Van Damme, Crombez, Hermans, & Koster, 2006).

Table 4.7. Three common post-extinction effects.

US ($\lambda = 0$, so $\lambda - V_T = 0 - 0 = 0$). Therefore, according to the Rescorla-Wagner model, pre-exposure to a novel CS without a US should be entirely irrelevant—but it is not.

Post-extinction (recovery) effects. Beside latent inhibition, a particularly salient limitation of the Rescorla-Wagner model is the prediction that extinction occurs because of a decline in associative strength—a sort of "unlearning." The empirical evidence shows that responding recovers easily after extinction, suggesting that the associative strength of the extinguished CS is preserved, but its behavioral expression is suppressed (Bouton, 2004). A wide range of changes in the environment may cause a recovery from extinction—these are called *post-extinction effects*. Table 4.7 lists the most reliable Pavlovian post-extinction effects. Post-extinction effects are of particular interest to those studying persistent behavior such as drug use and fearful responses (Kaplan, Heinrichs, & Carey, 2011).

There are a substantial number of effects that the Rescorla-Wagner model cannot explain (Miller, Barnet, & Grahame, 1995). Several theories have been developed to account for those effects (Mackintosh, 1975; Miller & Matzel, 1988; Pearce & Hall, 1980; Wagner, 2008). This does not mean that the Rescorla-Wagner model is a failure. On the contrary, it succeeds in explaining a large number of effects using a relatively simple algorithm and in identifying effects that require more complex algorithms. In doing this, it served as a launching pad for modern associative learning theories.

EXERCISES

1. For each of the following examples, indicate whether the contingency between stimuli is most likely positive, negative, or zero.

   a. The sight of the head of your best friend and the sight of one of his hands.
   b. Ingesting alcohol and feeling drunk.
   c. Seeing a green traffic light while driving and seeing pedestrians crossing the street in front of you.
   d. Hearing your favorite song and tasting bad milk.

2. An investigator wants to determine whether a transgenic strain of mice is capable of *trace* fear learning with arbitrary stimuli. Design a within-subject Pavlovian fear conditioning experiment to demonstrate this capability. Use either lights or tones as CS and mild foot shock as US. Specify the following:

   a. How would CS+ and CS– roles be assigned to each stimulus for each mouse?

b. Draw a horizontal timeline comprising an ITI and a trial. Indicate within that timeline the onset and duration of the CS–, CS+, and trace interval.

c. What test results would demonstrate fear conditioning?

3. Another investigator wants to know if the taste of a food (say, oranges) overshadows the smell of that food when developing a conditioned aversion to that odor. Design an overshadowing experiment to test this effect in rats, using lithium chloride to induce sickness. Specify the following:

a. The experimental and control training conditions.

b. What test results would demonstrate overshadowing?

4. Design an experiment to demonstrate whether taste may block smell when developing a conditioned aversion to that odor. Use the same stimuli as in Exercise 3; you will need to add a second odor. Specify the following:

a. The experimental and control training conditions.

b. What test results would demonstrate blocking?

5. Draw a graph tracking V_X as a function of trial for six trials. In trials one through three, the US was presented; trials four through six are extinction. Assume $V_{X,0} = 0$, $k = .05$, and $\lambda = 100$.

6. Using the overshadowing experimental design of Table 4.2, report V_A and V_B for the experimental and control conditions during testing. Assume three training trials, $V_{A,0} = V_{B,0} = 0$, $k = .05$, and $\lambda = 100$.

7. Using the blocking experimental design of Table 4.3, report V_C for the experimental and control conditions during testing. Assume three training trials in phase 1 and three training trials in phase 2, $V_{A,0} = V_{B,0} = V_{C,0} = 0$, $k = .05$, and $\lambda = 100$.

8. Demonstrate the over-expectation effect (Lattal & Nakajima, 1998) using the following experimental design:

CONDITION	TRAINING (PHASE 1)	TRAINING (PHASE 2)	TEST
Experimental	A+ / B+	AB+	S: A
Control	A+ / B+	CD+	R: ??

Assuming $V_{A,0} = V_{B,0} = 0$, under what condition (Experimental vs. Control) do you expect to see a stronger CR to A during testing? Show the calculations that led to your prediction.

9. Demonstrate the compound-extinction effect (Culver, Vervliet, & Craske, 2015) using the following experimental design:

CONDITION	TRAINING (PHASE 1)	TRAINING (PHASE 2)	TEST
Experimental	A+ / B+	AB–	S: A
Control	A+ / B+	A– / B–	R: ??

Assuming $V_{A,0} = V_{B,0} = 0$, under what condition (Experimental vs. Control) do you expect to see a stronger CR to A during testing? Show the calculations that led to your prediction.

REFERENCES

Arcediano, F., Matute, H., & Miller, R. R. (1997). Blocking of Pavlovian conditioning in humans. *Learning and Motivation, 28*(2), 188–199.

Besheer, J., Palmatier, M. I., Metschke, D. M., & Bevins, R. A. (2004). Nicotine as a signal for the presence or absence of sucrose reward: A Pavlovian drug appetitive conditioning preparation in rats. *Psychopharmacology, 172*(1), 108–117.

Bouton, M. E. (2004). Context and behavioral processes in extinction. *Learning & Memory, 11*(5), 485–494.

Bouton, M. E., & Bolles, R. C. (1980). Conditioned fear assessed by freezing and by the suppression of three different baselines. *Animal Learning & Behavior, 8*(3), 429–434.

Bouton, M. E., & King, D. A. (1983). Contextual control of the extinction of conditioned fear: Tests for the associative value of the context. *Journal of Experimental Psychology: Animal Behavior Processes, 9*(3), 248–265.

Brown, P. L., & Jenkins, H. M. (1968). Auto-shaping of the pigeon's key-peck. *Journal of the Experimental Analysis of Behavior, 11*, 1–8.

Christianson, J. P., Fernando, A. B. P., Kazama, A. M., Jovanovic, T., Ostroff, L. E., & Sangha, S. (2012). Inhibition of fear by learned safety signals: A mini-symposium review. *Journal of Neuroscience, 32*(41), 14118–14124.

Culver, N. C., Vervliet, B., & Craske, M. G. (2015). Compound extinction: Using the Rescorla-Wagner model to maximize exposure therapy effects for anxiety disorders. *Clinical Psychological Science, 3*(3), 335–348.

Daly, K. C., & Smith, B. H. (2000) Associative olfactory learning in the moth *Manduca sexta. Journal of Experimental Biology, 203*, 2025–2038.

Dielenberg, R. A., & McGregor, I. S. (2001). Defensive behavior in rats towards predatory odors: A review. *Neuroscience & Biobehavioral Reviews, 25*(7), 597–609.

Domjan, M. (2005). Pavlovian conditioning: A functional perspective. *Annual Review of Psychology, 56*, 179–206.

Domjan, M., Lyons, R., North, N. C., & Bruell, J. (1986). Sexual Pavlovian conditioned approach behavior in male Japanese quail (Coturnix coturnix japonica). *Journal of Comparative Psychology, 100*(4), 413–421.

Drew, M. R., Zupan, B., Cooke, A., Couvillon, P. A., & Balsam, P. D. (2005). Temporal control of conditioned responding in goldfish. *Journal of Experimental Psychology: Animal Behavior Processes, 31*(1), 31–39.

Estes, W. K., & Skinner, B. F. (1941). Some quantitative properties of anxiety. *Journal of Experimental Psychology, 29*(5), 390–400.

Flagel, S. B., Akil, H., & Robinson, T. E. (2009). Individual differences in the attribution of incentive salience to reward-related cues: Implications for addiction. *Neuropharmacology, 56*, 139–148.

Garcia, J., & Koelling, R. (1966). Relation of cue to consequence in avoidance learning. *Psychonomic Science, 4*(3), 123–124.

Gormezano, I., Schneiderman, N., Deaux, E., & Fuentes, I. (1962). Nictitating membrane: Classical conditioning and extinction in the albino rabbit. *Science, 138*(3536), 33–34.

Hearst, E., & Jenkins, H. M. (1974). *Sign-tracking: The stimulus-reinforcer relation and directed action.* Austin, TX: Psychonomic Society.

Holland, P. C. (1977). Conditioned stimulus as a determinant of the form of the Pavlovian conditioned response. *Journal of Experimental Psychology: Animal Behavior Processes, 3*(1), 77–104.

Holland, P. C. (1980). Influence of visual conditioned stimulus characteristics on the form of Pavlovian appetitive conditioned responding in rats. *Journal of Experimental Psychology: Animal Behavior Processes, 6*(1), 81–97.

Kamin, L. J. (1969). Predictability, surprise, attention, and conditioning. In B. A. Campbell & R. M. Church (Eds.), *Punishment and aversive behavior* (pp. 279–296). New York, NY: Appleton-Century-Crofts.

Kaplan, G. B., Heinrichs, S. C., & Carey, R. J. (2011). Treatment of addiction and anxiety using extinction approaches: Neural mechanisms and their treatment implications. *Pharmacology, Biochemistry and Behavior, 97*, 619–625.

Lattal, K. M., & Nakajima, S. (1998). Overexpectation in appetitive Pavlovian and instrumental conditioning. *Animal Learning & Behavior, 26*(3), 351–360.

Lissek, S., Biggs, A. L., Rabin, S. J., Cornwell, B. R., Alvarez, R. P., Pine, D. S., & Grillon, C. (2008). Generalization of conditioned fear-potentiated startle in humans: Experimental validation and clinical relevance. *Behaviour Research and Therapy, 46*(5), 678–687.

Lubow, R. E., & Gewirtz, J. C. (1995). Latent inhibition in humans: Data, theory, and implications for schizophrenia. *Psychological Bulletin, 117*(1), 87–103.

Lubow, R. E., & Weiner, I. (2010). *Latent inhibition: Cognition, neuroscience and applications to schizophrenia.* Cambridge, UK: Cambridge University Press.

Mackintosh, N. J. (1975). A theory of attention: Variations in the associability of stimuli with reinforcement. *Psychological Review, 82*(4), 276–298.

Maren, S. (2001). Neurobiology of Pavlovian fear conditioning. *Annual Review of Neuroscience, 24*(1), 897–931.

Miller, R. R., Barnet, R., & Grahame, N. (1995). Assessment of the Rescorla-Wagner model. *Psychological Bulletin, 117*, 363.

Miller, R. R., & Matzel, L. D. (1988). The comparator hypothesis: A response rule for the expression of associations. *Psychology of Learning and Motivation, 22*, 51–92.

Miller, R. R., & Spear, N. E. (1985). *Information processing in animals: Conditioned inhibition.* Hillsdale, NJ: Lawrence Erlbaum.

Papini, M. R., & Bitterman, M. E. (1990). The role of contingency in classical conditioning. *Psychological Review, 97*(3), 396–403.

Pearce, J. M. (1987). A model for stimulus generalization in Pavlovian conditioning. *Psychological Review, 94*(1), 61–73.

Pearce, J. M., & Hall, G. (1980). A model for Pavlovian learning: Variations in the effectiveness of conditioned but not of unconditioned stimuli. *Psychological Review, 87*(6), 532–552.

Rau, V., & Fanselow, M. S. (2007). Neurobiological and neuroethological perspectives on fear and anxiety. In L. J. Kirmayer, R. Lemelson, & M. Barad (Eds.), *Understanding trauma: Integrating biological, clinical, and cultural perspectives* (pp. 27–40). Cambridge, UK: Cambridge University Press.

Rescorla, R. A. (1967a). Inhibition of delay in Pavlovian fear conditioning. *Journal of Comparative and Physiological Psychology, 64*(1), 114–120.

Rescorla, R. A. (1967b). Pavlovian conditioning and its proper control procedures. *Psychological Review, 74*(1), 71–80.

Rescorla, R. A. (1969). Pavlovian conditioned inhibition. *Psychological Bulletin, 72*(2), 77–94.

Rescorla, R. A. (2004). Spontaneous recovery. *Learning & Memory, 11*(5), 501–509.

Rescorla, R. A., & Wagner, A. R. (1972). A theory of Pavlovian conditioning. In A. Black & W. Prokasy (Eds.), *Classical Conditioning, II* (pp. 64–99). New York, NY: Appleton-Century-Crofts.

Savastano, H. I., Cole, R. P., Barnet, R. C., & Miller, R. R. (1999). Reconsidering conditioned inhibition. *Learning and Motivation, 30*(1), 101–127.

Savastano, H. I., & Miller, R. R. (1998). Time as content in Pavlovian conditioning. *Behavioural Processes, 44*(2), 147–162.

Sears, L. L., Finn, P. R., & Steinmetz, J. E. (1994). Abnormal classical eye-blink conditioning in autism. *Journal of Autism and Developmental Disorders, 24*(6), 737–751.

Silva, K. M., & Timberlake, W. (1998). The organization and temporal properties of appetitive behavior in rats. *Learning & Behavior, 26*(2), 182–195.

Solomon, P. R., Vander Schaaf, E. R., Thompson, R. F., & Weisz, D. J. (1986). Hippocampus and trace conditioning of the rabbit's classically conditioned nictitating membrane response. *Behavioral Neuroscience, 100*(5), 729–744.

Tzschentke, T. M. (2007). Measuring reward with the conditioned place preference (CPP) paradigm: Update of the last decade. *Addiction Biology, 12*, 227–462.

Uslaner, J. M., Acerbo, M. J., Jones, S. A., & Robinson, T. E. (2006). The attribution of incentive salience to a stimulus that signals an intravenous injection of cocaine. *Behavioural Brain Research, 169*(2), 320–324.

Van Damme, S., Crombez, G., Hermans, D., & Koster, E. H. W. (2006). The role of extinction and reinstatement in attentional bias to threat: A conditioning approach. *Behaviour Research and Therapy, 44*(11), 1555–1563.

Van Hest, A., Van Haaren, F., Kop, P., & Van der Schoot, F. (1986). Stimulus-and feeder-directed behavior in a long-box: Effect of fixed versus variable time schedules of food presentation. *Animal Learning & Behavior, 14*(2), 168–172.

Wagner, A. R. (2008). Evolution of an elemental theory of Pavlovian conditioning. *Learning & Behavior, 36*(3), 253–265.

Weike, A. I., Schupp, H. T., & Hamm, A. O. (2007). Fear acquisition requires awareness in trace but not delay conditioning. *Psychophysiology, 44*(1), 170–180.

Welzl, H., D'Adamo, P., & Lipp, H. P. (2001). Conditioned taste aversion as a learning and memory paradigm. *Behavioural Brain Research, 125*(1), 205–213.

Williams, D. A., Overmier, J. B., & LoLordo, V. M. (1992). A reevaluation of Rescorla's early dictums about Pavlovian conditioned inhibition. *Psychological Bulletin, 111*(2), 275–290.

Image Credits

Fig 4.1a: Source: https://pixabay.com/en/according-to-sound-speakers-volume-214445.

Fig. 4.1b: Copyright © Ralvarezlara00 (CC BY-SA 3.0) at https://commons.wikimedia.org/wiki/File:Aspect_of_several_iberulites.jpg.

Fig. 4.1c: Source: https://pixabay.com/en/eye-eyelash-optic-optical-organ-2027337.

FUNDAMENTALS OF OPERANT CONDITIONING

In Pavlovian conditioning, the organism responds to a regularity in the environment—the temporal relation between two stimuli (the CS and the US). In that situation, the response from the organism does not affect the relation between the two stimuli. Whether the rat freezes in a fear-conditioning paradigm does not affect the presentation of the tone CS or of the foot shock US. In Pavlovian conditioning, the organism learns about the relation between two stimuli, but it can only learn one thing about the relation between the organism's own behavior and stimuli: that its behavior cannot affect the environment. When the stimulus that is impervious to behavior is aversive, such learning is called *learned helplessness* (Maier & Seligman, 1976). Learned helplessness appears to model important aspects of clinical depression (Pryce et al., 2011).

Of course, there are many other ways in which behavior and stimuli may be related, aside from one not affecting the other. A response may increase the probability of a stimulus, or it may reduce it. The movement of a predator to a particular location may increase the probability of encountering prey; the probability of consuming a drug is reduced during therapy. When the response changes because of its effect on a stimulus, we call such change *operant* or *instrumental* conditioning. More specifically, operant conditioning is the change in the frequency or probability of a response, caused by a change in the consequence or outcome of that response. Such change in the response shows that the organism has learned that its behavior causes a change in the environment.

In the laboratory, two archetypal operant conditioning paradigms are the rat pressing a lever for food and the pigeon pecking a key for food. In both cases, a response that has a low probability prior to training (pressing a lever, pecking a key) increases in probability because of its outcome: food. The similarity between sign-tracking (Chapter 4) and operant pecking may help in drawing a contrast between Pavlovian and operant conditioning. In both cases a stimulus—the illuminated key—is presented, it is pecked, and it is followed by food. However, in Pavlovian conditioning, the key-light and food occur irrespective of whether pecking occurs, and pecking occurs because the key-light and food are paired. In operant conditioning, the food occurs because the key-light is pecked, and pecking occurs because, in the presence of the key-light, it produces food. There is, indeed, a pairing of the key-light and food in operant key-pecking, but the experimenter does not control such pairing; instead, the key-pecking response mediates it.

Whereas Pavlovian learning involves the association between stimuli, operant learning involves the association between responses and stimuli. To highlight this distinction, think about a natural Pavlovian learning situation and turn it into an operant learning situation. For instance, a red traffic light at a busy intersection (one stimulus) is associated with cars crossing in front of the driver (another stimulus); running a red traffic light (a response) is associated with a higher probability of an accident (another stimulus, the outcome of the response), which reduces the probability of running a red light. In the box, describe an example of a Pavlovian learning situation and a closely related operant learning situation.

Box 5.1

Pavlovian learning situation   Operant learning situation

Stimulus 1:   Response:

Stimulus 2:   Outcome:

BASIC CONCEPTS

Experimental design and contingency. Operant conditioning is an experimental procedure that demonstrates a *causal relation* between an outcome (e.g., food) and future instances of the behavior that produced that outcome (e.g., pressing a lever). Two variables define this causal relation: the response-outcome relation (pressing a lever produces food) and the probability of that response. Therefore, in operant conditioning, the independent variable is the presence/absence of the response-outcome relation and the dependent variable is the probability of the response.

Operant conditioning is typically demonstrated by comparing the probability of a response when it produces the outcome relative to when it does not. To the extent that food maintains lever-pressing, the removal of food should result in a decline in lever-pressing. This approach, however, has the limitation of confounding the response-outcome relation with the outcome itself. This is a particularly important problem when the outcome is the intravenous administration of a psychostimulant, such as cocaine or amphetamine. Psychostimulants sensitize locomotor behavior (Stewart & Badiani, 1993), which may be expressed as an increase in the target response. In such a case, the increase in the probability of the response is not due to operant conditioning, nor is it due to the response resulting in the psychostimulant; instead, it is due to the psychostimulant sensitizing the response. Alternatively, if training takes place for short periods of time in the same context, or if some stimulus precedes presentation of the psychostimulant, that context or that stimulus may serve as a CS (for the psychostimulants US) that elicits the target response. In such a case, the increase in the probability of the response is not due to operant conditioning, but to the response becoming a Pavlovian CR. A change in response probability in the presence of an outcome, but not because the response *produces* the outcome, is called *operant pseudoconditioning*.

The *yoked-control* design distinguishes between operant conditioning and pseudoconditioning (Figure 5.1). In the yoked-control design, the target response may be emitted in the experimental and control conditions, but only responses in the experimental condition produce the outcome in both conditions. Consider, for instance, a between-subject experiment to demonstrate that the intravenous administration of a novel drug may serve as an operant outcome, increasing the response that produces it. In this design, a group of rats (called *master*) is assigned to the experimental condition and another group of rats (called *yoked*) is assigned to the control condition. Each time a master rat presses a lever, it produces an intravenous administration of the drug to itself and also to an assigned yoked rat. Yoked rats also have access to a lever,

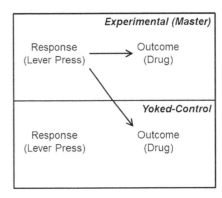

Figure 5.1. Schematic representation of the yoked-control design, illustrated with a between-subject design of drug reinforcement.

but their lever-pressing does not produce the drug. Note that master and yoked rats experience similar training conditions (same stimuli, including the drug presented with similar frequencies). However, the drug is *contingent* on lever-pressing for master rats and is *non-contingent* for yoked rats. Therefore, systematic differences in response frequency between master and yoked rats can only be attributed to the response-outcome contingency. Such a difference demonstrates operant learning.

An alternative to the between-subject yoked-control is the within-subject design, in which experimental and control conditions alternate for every subject. In the within-subject yoked-control procedure, responses in the experimental condition produce the outcome in both the experimental (contingent) and in the control (non-contingent) conditions; responses in the control condition are ineffective (Church, 1989).

Subjects and equipment. Similar to Pavlovian conditioning, operant conditioning is studied in a wide variety of species, including invertebrates (Brembs, 2003), but the most common species are small rodents and birds. Particularly for rodents, operant conditioning may be implemented on a wide range of standard equipment, including running wheels (running in the wheel makes it turn), land mazes (finding a goal box results in food), water mazes (finding a submerged platform allows the animal to rest from swimming), and, more typically, small enclosures called *Skinner boxes* (after B. F. Skinner, see Chapter 1). When appetitive outcomes are involved, the Skinner box includes keys or levers with which subjects may interact; these are called *manipulanda* (singular, *manipulandum*). A common apparatus to study operant conditioning with aversive outcomes in rodents is the *active-avoidance shuttle-box*. The shuttle-box is similar to the conditioned place preference (CPP) apparatus (Chapter 4), with the dividing door kept open and furbished with auditory and visual stimuli than can be turned on and off. The floor in each side of the box can be independently electrified to deliver foot-shock. One side (the shock side) is sometimes electrified, while the other side (the safe side) is not. Shock- and safe-side assignments may vary during a training session, typically depending on the location of the animal; auditory and visual stimuli may indicate this assignment. By moving from the shock side to the safe side (or *shuttling*), the animal reduces exposure to footshock.

Unlike work with more typical laboratory animals, operant research with humans and non-traditional species relies on equipment developed by the investigators. Human operant research is typically conducted on videogame-like interfaces, using controllers and keyboards for collecting responses and points exchangeable for prizes or money as outcomes. Joysticks and touchscreen devices are fairly common in operant research with non-human primates.

Measuring behavior. Operant conditioning is assessed using one of two types of procedures: *discrete-trials* and *free-operant* procedures. The discrete-trials procedure restricts access to a manipulandum, and the response can only be emitted once per opportunity. In this procedure, the probability of a response is the number of responses emitted per opportunity to respond. For instance, the onset of a small light may signal, to a rat, the beginning of a trial in an active-avoidance shuttle-box. The trial ends once the rat either receives shock or shuttles to the safe side and avoids shock. In this example, the probability of a response is the proportion of trials in which shuttling occurs.

In the free-operant procedure, the manipulandum is continually available. Response probability cannot be computed from the proportion of trials with a response because there are no discrete trials. Instead, response probability is estimated indirectly, through the *response rate*, which will be signified with the letter B (other symbols and abbreviations are included in Table 5.1). B is a surrogate for response probability and is the key dependent measure of operant conditioning (Skinner, 1938); it is the number of responses produced per unit of time.

Response rate is often estimated using the *cumulative record* (Ferster and Skinner, 1957). The cumulative record is obtained from a drum (or cumulative) recorder, which draws a continuous horizontal line at a constant speed, shifts upward by a small fixed distance with each response, and resets when it meets the edge of the drum (Figure 5.2). Every time the outcome is delivered, the event is marked on the line with a tick or harsh mark.

The slope of the cumulative record is the response rate over a period of time. The absence of responses over a period of time is expressed as a flat horizontal line over that period. When responses are emitted at a very high rate, the record rises quickly, drawing a very steep line. In fact, if each vertical change in the cumulative record is represented as a fraction of total responses (e.g., if there are 1,000 responses total, each vertical change = 1/1,000), the cumulative record is an empirical cumulative distribution function of responses over time. The slope, at any given time, of this modified cumulative record is an estimate of the probability of a response at that time.

In Box 5.2 (page 68), draw a cumulative record similar to that of Figure 5.2, in which the organism produced, on average, 10 responses per min ($B = 10$ resp/min) for five minutes. Do not mark the delivery of outcomes and disregard detailed, local changes in response rate, but do not forget to include axis labels and units.

Cumulative records are rarely obtained from drum recorders anymore. Instead, responses are typically recorded electronically, through a computer interface that also controls the stimuli in the experimental environment. Cumulative records are now produced electronically, such as the one simulated in Figure 5.2.

The three-term contingency. Like any other behavior, operant behavior does not occur in a void. In fact, a key aspect of the context in which operant conditioning takes place is the stimulus that signals that a particular response will produce a particular outcome. This may be, for instance, a small light in the Skinner box indicating that pressing a lever will yield food. This stimulus is called the *discriminative stimulus* and is signified as S^D (*"S-dee"*). Note that in the yoked-control design (Figure 5.1), the S^D is present in both the experimental and yoked-control conditions, but it only signals the response-outcome relation in the experimental condition. To differentiate it from stimuli that unconditionally elicit the target response, the S^D is said to *set the occasion* for that response.

Prior to operant-conditioning training—that is, before the operant response produces the target outcome—the rate at which a response is emitted in the presence of the to-be S^D is the *operant level* of that response. Operant conditioning is implemented on that response when it produces the outcome only in the presence of the S^D. The efficacy of operant conditioning is often measured as the difference between the operant response rate in the presence of the S^D and its operant level. This measure has an important limitation: The operant level does not involve the non-contingent presentation of the outcome, so it is vulnerable to pseudoconditioning.

SYMBOL/ABBREVIATION	MEANING
Responses	
B	Response rate
IRT	Inter-response time
Stimuli	
S^D	Discriminative stimulus
S^Δ	A stimulus in the presence of which the response does not produce the target outcome
S^{r+}	Reinforcer (appetitive)
S^{p+}	Punisher (aversive)
S^{r-}	Stimulus removed by a negatively-reinforced response (aversive)
S^{p-}	Stimulus removed by a negatively-punished response (appetitive)
Schedules of Reinforcement	
DRO (DRA)	Differential reinforcement of other (alternative) behavior
CRF	Continuous reinforcement (also, FR1)
FR	Fixed-ratio schedule
VR	Variable-ratio schedule
RR	Random-ratio schedule
FI	Fixed-interval schedule
LH	Limited hold
VI	Variable-interval schedule
RI	Random-interval schedule
DRL	Differential reinforcement of low rates
DRH	Differential reinforcement of high rates
NCR	Non-contingent reinforcement
FT	Fixed-time schedule
VT	Variable-time schedule
Schedule Parameters	
n	Mean ratio requirement
T	Mean interval requirement
R	Rate of reinforcement

Table 5.1. Symbols and abbreviations.

Box 5.2

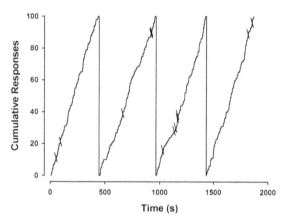

Figure 5.2. A (simulated) cumulative record on a 100-response wide drum. The hash marks indicate the delivery of an outcome.

Operant Conditioning

Figure 5.3. Schematic representation of the three-term contingency. The discriminative stimulus (S^D, or antecedent) sets the occasion for a response (or behavior) that produces an outcome (or consequence). The outcome changes the probability of the response in the presence of the S^D.

The S^D (or *antecedent*), the operant response (or behavior), and the outcome of that response (or consequence) constitute the *three-term contingency* (Figure 5.3) (Davison & Nevin, 1999). The first letters of the components of the three-term contingency—Antecedent, Behavior, and Consequence, or ABC—provide a mnemonic aid. The three-term contingency is the general rule that, in the presence of S^D A, response B (not to be confused with response *rate B*) will produce outcome C.

In Box 5.1, you identified two of the three components of an operant learning situation, a response and an outcome, but you left out the S^D. What would constitute the S^D in that example? Identify the S^D, along with the response and outcome, in Box 5.3.

The operant response is often defined in terms of its effect on the environment. For instance, *key-pecking* is often defined as the closure of a micro-switch in the back of the key. When defined this way, the response is called an *operant*. Note that the key-pecking operant does not indicate how the micro-switch is closed or exactly how much force is impinged upon the key. The operant is a *class* of responses that have a common effect on the environment. The operant involves two categories: It either occurs (the micro-switch is closed) or it does not (the micro-switch is open). In contrast, the particular action that results in the operant, called the *topography* of the operant response, involves a potentially infinite number of categories (e.g., pecking with beak open or closed, pecking at a particular part of the key, etc.)

Box 5.3

S^D (**A**ntecendent):

Response (**B**ehavior):

Outcome (**C**onsequence):

For your example in Box 5.3, indicate two different response topographies that would have resulted in the same outcome. These topographies constitute members of the same operant class.

Box 5.4

Topography 1:

Topography 2:

A stimulus in whose presence the operant does *not* result in the outcome is an S$^\Delta$ (*"S-delta"*). The operant is a *discriminated operant* when response rate B varies depending on whether the S^D or the S$^\Delta$ is present. The discriminated operant demonstrates that the organism can detect the difference between the S^D and the S$^\Delta$, which implies a particular sensory capacity. For instance, if you turn on and off a light fast enough, you see it as a steady light. Every time your television refreshes the image on the screen you do not see a flickering of lights, but a continuous change in an image. A discriminated operant may be implemented to establish, in many species, the flicker-fusion threshold, which is the refreshment rate at which such flickering is just perceived (e.g., Woo et al., 2009).

For your example in Box 5.3, is there a stimulus that explicitly indicates that the response will *not* result in the outcome and would thus constitute an S$^\Delta$? If so, describe it in the Box 5.5; otherwise, write "None."

Box 5.5

S$^\Delta$:

Reinforcement and punishment. The outcome of the response may increase or reduce response rate *B*. The outcome is a *reinforcer* if it increases *B*, and a *punisher* if it reduces *B*. Reinforcement and punishment may involve the introduction or the removal of a stimulus. Figure 5.4 classifies operant procedures according to whether the outcome is the introduction or reduction of a stimulus, and according to its effect on *B*. In *positive reinforcement* and *positive punishment* (more often referred to simply as *punishment*), the response increases the probability of a stimulus that is either appetitive (a *reinforcer*, or S^{r+}) or aversive (a *punisher*, or S^{p+}). An example of positive reinforcement is the increased pressing of a lever in a hungry animal because pressing the lever produces food; food is the S^{r+}. An example of punishment is a reduction in lever-pressing because it leads to foot shock; foot shock is the S^{p+}.

In *negative reinforcement*, the removal of an aversive stimulus S^{r-} increases *B*. Negative reinforcement procedures are classified in two categories: *escape* (or *passive avoidance*) and *active avoidance*. In the *escape* procedure, the response removes the S^{r-} *after* its onset; in the *active avoidance* procedure, the response removes the S^{r-} *before* its onset. For example, a rat is escaping foot shock when it traverses the shuttle-box to the safe side while foot shock is delivered; a rat is actively avoiding foot shock when it traverses the shuttle-box during a tone that signals imminent foot shock. As you can see, active avoidance is similar to fear conditioning (Chapter 4), but allows the rat to move away from the S^{r-} before

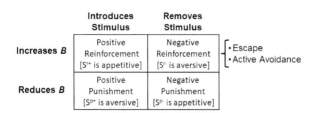

Figure 5.4. Classification of operant procedures in terms of the nature of the outcome (it *introduces* versus *removes* a stimulus) and of its impact on rate of response (it increases versus reduces *B*). Two negative-reinforcement procedures are highlighted: passive avoidance (escape) and active avoidance.

it is presented. In our active-avoidance example, the tone (S^D) sets the occasion for the rat to traverse the shuttle-box, which is reinforced with the absence of foot shock.

Although escape and active avoidance are adaptive responses to threats, active avoidance can lead to particularly disruptive behavior. Suppose that in the shuttle-box example, foot shock was no longer delivered. Such change would not affect the experience of a rat that learned to avoid shock—when the tone is presented, traversing the shuttle-box would result in no foot shock (of course, not traversing the shuttle-box would also result in no foot shock). It is thus not surprising that avoidance behavior

CHAPTER 5: FUNDAMENTALS OF OPERANT CONDITIONING | 71

often persists despite the discontinuation of the S^{r-} (Solomon, Kamin, & Wynne, 1953). Such persistence appears to model key aspects of phobias and anxiety disorders (Dymond & Roche, 2009) and has informed strategies for their treatment (Levis & Krantweiss, 2003).

In *negative punishment*, the response removes an appetitive stimulus S^{p-}, which reduces B. Negative punishment is a common procedure for reducing undesired behavior in children, such as acting out (Petscher, Rey, & Bailey, 2009). In that situation, the undesired behavior removes an appetitive S^{p-} (e.g., attention from caregiver), and thus reduces the rate of the undesired behavior. Depending on their specific implementation, negative-punishment procedures take different names such as *omission training*, *differential reinforcement of other behavior* (or DRO), or *differential reinforcement of alternative behavior* (or DRA). In the DRO, for instance, an appetitive stimulus is delivered only if the response is not emitted for a period of time.

To what type of operant procedure does your example in Box 5.3 correspond? Answer the questions in Box 5.6 and match those answers to the matrix of Figure 5.4 to determine the corresponding operant procedure.

Box 5.6

Does the outcome involve the introduction or the removal of a stimulus? Identify the stimulus next to your answer.

    (a) Introduction of _____   (b) Removal of _____

Do you expect the outcome to increase or reduce the probability of future responses?

    (a) Increase   (b) Reduce

Based on your answers, what type of operant procedure corresponds to your example?

    (a) Positive reinforcement   (b) Positive punishment

    (c) Negative reinforcement   (d) Negative punishment

Based on your answers, is the stimulus in your example appetitive or aversive?

    (a) Appetitive   (b) Aversive

Despite the broad range of operant conditioning procedures, positive reinforcement is the most frequently implemented procedure. The remainder of this book will, therefore, focus on this procedure.

SIMPLE SCHEDULES OF REINFORCEMENT

Contingencies of reinforcement. When a response produces an outcome, it is said that the outcome is contingent on the response. If, in addition, the response-outcome contingency increases B, then it is said that the outcome reinforces the response—it is a S^{r+}. The rules by which a response produces a reinforcer are called the *contingencies of reinforcement*. Contingencies of reinforcement may be thought of as models of naturally occurring positive feedback loops between behavior and environment (e.g., between foraging behavior and preys obtained), or as techniques to promote behavior at desired levels (e.g., engaging in play behavior at moderate levels).

The simplest contingency of reinforcement is *continuous reinforcement*, or CRF, where every response is reinforced. A more formal way of defining CRF is as $p(S^{r+}|\text{response}) = 1.0$ (the probability of the reinforcer given the behavior is 1.0). *Intermittent reinforcement*, on the other hand, involves reinforcing only some instances of the response: $0.0 < p(S^{r+}|\text{response}) < 1.0$. Whereas there is only one way to implement CRF, there are an infinite number of ways to implement intermittent reinforcement. This section reviews simple contingencies of reinforcement, intermittent and otherwise; these contingencies are arranged as a matrix in Figure 5.5. Ferster and Skinner (1957) first described most of these schedules. All schedules are described in terms of required responses and time; in all schedules, responses and time only count while the S^D is present.

Ratio schedules. In *ratio* schedules of reinforcement, S^{r+} is contingent on completing a *ratio requirement*, which is a number of responses (*n*) since the last reinforcer. When $n = 1$, the schedule is CRF. When $n > 1$, the requirement may be fixed or variable (Figure 5.5). For instance, in a *fixed-ratio* (FR) 10 schedule, a pigeon may be required to peck a key 10 times to obtain S^{r+}. Completing an FR schedule is akin to paying a price *n* for each S^{r+}, where the responses are the currency of payment. In fact, the FR schedule is a key tool for understanding conditioning from an economic perspective, an approach known as *behavioral economics* (Bickel, Johnson, Koffarnus, McKillop, & Murphy, 2014; see also Chapter 6).

In Box 5.7, draw a hypothetical cumulative record (similar to the one in Figure 5.2) that depicts performance on an FR 20 schedule of reinforcement, implemented in a 30-minute training session. Make sure to include axis labels and units; use hash marks to indicate the delivery of reinforcement. On average, what was the rate of response (*B*) in your example? What was the rate of reinforcement (*r*)? Don't forget to include units for your estimates.

	Fixed	Variable
Ratio	Fixed Ratio (FR)	Variable Ratio (VR)
Interval	Fixed Interval (FI)	Variable Interval (VI)

Figure 5.5. Simple schedules of (positive) reinforcement classified according to whether its requirement is a number of responses (*ratio*) or the first response after an interval (*interval*), and whether it is the same (*fixed*) or different (*variable*) between reinforcers.

Box 5.7

Average *B*: _____   Average *r*: _____

In *variable-ratio* (VR) schedules, $n > 1$ and the requirement changes unsystematically between S^{r+}; n is the *mean* requirement. For instance, in a VR 10 schedule, a rat may obtain S^{r+} by pressing a lever 5, 10, or 15 times, where no cue indicates which requirement is currently effective. Ratio requirements may be sampled, with or without replacement, from an arithmetic progression (equally-spaced numbers) with mean n. In such a sampling method, however, the probability of reinforcement given x responses since the last reinforcer, $p(S^{r+}|x)$, increases with x [in the VR 10 example, $p(S^{r+}|5) = .33$, $p(S^{r+}|10) = .50$, and $p(S^{r+}|10) = 1.0$]. To keep $p(S^{r+}|x)$ constant over x, investigators often rely on *random-ratio* (or RR) schedules of reinforcement, in which every response is reinforced with probability p, where $p = 1/n$. In a RR 10 schedule, each response would be reinforced with $p = .10$. It is important to be aware that RR schedules may yield very large ratio requirements, which may not support responses; this is known as *ratio strain*. In a RR 10 schedule there is, for instance, one chance in 37,658 that the next requirement will be greater than 100. If FR schedules are like paying a fixed price for a good, VR and RR schedules are like playing the lottery, where each ticket costs one response that has a $1/n$ probability of winning.

Paying for goods and playing the lottery are everyday behavior-environment interactions that ratio schedules model well, because they involve a positive feedback relation between behavior and outcomes: The more you pay, the more goods you get; the more lottery tickets you buy, the more likely you are to win. In Box 5.8, describe an example of a typical behavior-environment interaction that has a positive feedback relation that is well modeled by ratio schedules. Would your example be best modeled by an FR or a VR schedule?

Box 5.8

Interval schedules. In *interval* schedules of reinforcement, the next S^{r+} is contingent on emitting one response after some time *t* has elapsed since the last S^{r+}. The *interval requirement t* is never signaled (otherwise the signal would be an S^Δ). Responses prior to *t* are not reinforced. Like ratio requirements, interval requirements may be fixed or variable (Figure 5.5, bottom row). For instance, in a *fixed-interval* (FI) 3-min schedule, the first press of the lever after three minutes have elapsed is reinforced. The FI schedule is akin to boiling water in a pot. If it takes five minutes for the water to boil, checking the pot before five minutes have elapsed does not result in the boiling water S^{r+}; only checking it after five minutes is reinforced with boiled water.

In Box 5.9, draw a hypothetical cumulative record that depicts performance on an FI 100-s schedule of reinforcement, implemented in a 30-minute training session. Make sure to include axis labels and units; use hash marks to indicate the delivery of reinforcement. On average, what was the rate of response (*B*) in your example? What was the rate of reinforcement (*r*)?

Box 5.9

Average *B*: _____   Average *r*: _____

In the boiling water example, however, waiting too long (e.g., 30 minutes) probably results in no water: It has all boiled away. Such constraint on the availability of the S^{r+} may be incorporated to an FI schedule as a *limited hold* or LH. The LH is the maximum time after t during which the reinforcer is available. In the boiling water example, if the water was boiled away after 30 minutes, the boiling water S^{r+} may reinforce the checking behavior on an FI 5-min LH 25-min schedule. To avoid missing the LH window, or simply because S^{r+} is typically preferred sooner rather than later, people often use a kitchen timer to signal when to check what they are cooking. FI performance, in the absence of such external timers, is thus a useful indicator of the control that time exerts over reinforced behavior (Daniels & Sanabria, 2017; Henderson, Hurly, Bateson, & Healy, 2006).

In *variable-interval* (VI) schedules, the interval requirement changes between S^{r+} deliveries. For instance, in a VI 60-s schedule a rat may obtain S^{r+} by pressing a lever after 30, 60, or 90 seconds have elapsed, where $t = 60$ seconds is the mean interval requirement. Interval requirements may be sampled, with or without replacement, from an arithmetic progression (equally-spaced times) with mean t. In such a sampling method, however, the probability of reinforcement, given that interval y has elapsed since the last reinforcer, $(S^{r+}|y)$, increases with y [see the explanation for $p(S^{r+}|x)$ for an arithmetic progression of ratio requirements in the *Ratio Schedules* section]. To keep $p(S^{r+}|t)$ approximately constant, investigators often rely on a *random-interval* (or RI) schedule, in which the interval requirement may be completed, with probability p, after every interval τ ("tau"), where τ is typically short and fixed (e.g., 1 second); $p = \tau / t$. It is important to be aware that RI schedules may yield very long interval requirements, which may not support responding (*interval strain*). A method that keeps $p(S^{r+}|t)$ approximately constant and prevents interval strain is sampling, with or without replacement, from a *Fleshler-Hoffman progression* of intervals (Fleshler & Hoffman, 1962). In this progression, longer intervals are more spaced from each other than shorter intervals, such that the distribution of sampled intervals approximates the exponential distribution of requirements expected from a constant $p(S^{r+}|y)$.

Variable- and random-interval schedules are akin to the delivery of important email messages to your inbox. Each important email message arrives to your inbox at an unpredictable time; until such a time, checking your inbox will not be reinforced with an important email message. As soon as an important email message arrives, checking your inbox just once allows you to read that message, which reinforces checking your inbox.

Waiting for water to boil or for an email message to arrive are everyday behavior-environment interactions that interval schedules model well, because they involve a minimal relation between behavior and outcomes: Waiting a while for your water to boil will not give you more boiling water; checking your inbox every second is unlikely to provide you with more important messages. In Box 5.10, describe an example of a behavior-environment interaction that has the minimal relation that is well modeled by interval schedules. Would your example be best modeled by an FI or a VI schedule?

Box 5.10

Other simple schedules. The matrix of Figure 5.5 organizes fairly common and simple schedules of reinforcement on the basis of two characteristics: whether the rate of reinforcement depends primarily on behavior (ratio) or on time (interval). Of course, not all schedules of reinforcement fit in that matrix.

The *differential reinforcement of low rates* (DRL) schedule is usually implemented to train or assess the capacity to respond at a slow pace (e.g., Sanabria & Killeen, 2008). In this schedule, S^{r+} is contingent on a minimum interval (e.g., 6 seconds) between consecutive responses (inter-response time, or IRT). Similar to FI schedules, an LH may be implemented in DRL, such that IRTs longer than the LH are not reinforced. The opposite of DRL, the *differential reinforcement of high rates* (DRH), is often implemented to train a fast pace of responding. In DRH, S^{r+} is contingent on IRTs shorter than a criterion.

At operant level, organisms oftentimes do not emit the would-be operant, making it difficult for the organism to experience the contingencies of reinforcement once they are implemented. For instance, at operant level, a rat may not press a lever with more than 20 grams of force, not because it is not physically capable of doing it, but simply because it does not appear in its spontaneous behavior. This would make it very difficult to train lever-pressing under any schedule. A *shaping* procedure may be used to address this challenge and put behavior in contact with the contingencies of reinforcement. Shaping involves the selective reinforcement of successive approximations to a target response (e.g., pressing a lever). A particularly systematic shaping procedure is the *percentile* schedule of reinforcement (Galbicka, 1994). Reinforcement in this schedule is contingent on a quantifiable dimension of behavior meeting a criterion that adjusts on the basis of recent performance. The rat in the previous example may be trained on a percentile schedule that only reinforces lever presses with force greater than the median of the last 15 lever presses. This is expected to progressively increase the force of lever presses toward the 20-gram target.

Non-contingent reinforcement and extinction. *Non-contingent reinforcement* (or NCR) and *extinction* are better described as schedules of *non*-reinforcement. In NCR, an otherwise contingent S^{r+} is delivered in a non-contingent way. The yoked-control condition (bottom of Figure 5.1) is an example of NCR. *Time* schedules also involve NCR. Time schedules are similar to interval schedules but without the response requirement: Once the interval requirement is completed, the stimulus that would serve as S^{r+} is immediately delivered. Like interval schedules, time schedules can be fixed (FT) or variable (VT).[1]

In Box 5.11, draw a hypothetical cumulative record that depicts performance in a 30-minute training session, organized like this: FR 50 during the first 10 minutes, FT 60-s during the following 10 minutes, and FI 60-s during the last 10 minutes. Use hash marks to indicate the delivery of reinforcement, whether contingent or not.

Box 5.11

_____

Whereas in NCR the response-S^{r+} contingency is removed, in operant extinction the S^{r+} is removed altogether. More specifically, operant extinction is the decline of B because of the discontinuation of the S^{r+}. The post-extinction effects observed in Pavlovian conditioning (Chapter 4) are also observed in operant conditioning (Bouton, Winterbauer, & Todd, 2012). A pause in extinction training (removing the S^D and then presenting it again) recovers the response (spontaneous recovery; Rescorla, 1997). When training is conducted in one context (S^D) and is then extinguished in a different context (S^Δ), a return to the original context, or a simple change of context, recovers the response (renewal; Bouton, Todd, Vurbic, & Winterbauer, 2011). NCR recovers the extinguished response as well (reinstatement; Franks & Lattal, 1976). The reacquisition of an extinguished response is typically faster than its first acquisition (rapid reacquisition; Willcocks & McNally, 2011). In addition, the extinction of a response often promotes the recovery of a response extinguished in the same context (Lieving & Lattal, 2003; Winterbauer & Bouton, 2010). This operant post-extinction effect is known as *resurgence*; for a Pavlovian analogue of resurgence, see Kearns and Weiss (2007). Taken together, these effects suggest that, similar to Pavlovian extinction, operant extinction does not involve the *unlearning* of the reinforced response, but instead involves the acquisition of a context-dependent suppression of the expression of the reinforced response.

In Box 5.12, draw a hypothetical cumulative record that depicts performance in *two* 15-minute training sessions, conducted on separate days. In Session 1, VI 120-s is implemented during the first 10 minutes, and extinction during the last 5 minutes. In Session 2, extinction is implemented throughout. Make sure you show the spontaneous recovery effect at the beginning of Session 2.

---

1 "Non-contingent reinforcement" appears to be a contradiction in terms: a defining characteristic of the S^{r+} is that it is contingent to the response. This terminology has persisted, however, because performance in NCR is typically compared to performance in schedules in which the S^{r+} is contingent.

Box 5.12

Schedule control and feedback functions. The cumulative records you drew in the previous section probably showed relatively constant rates of response while contingent reinforcement was delivered. They were also probably very similar, regardless of whether the schedule was FR or VI. In actuality, as shown in the illustrative cumulative records in Figure 5.6, schedules of reinforcement do not always yield constant rates of responding, and they vary substantially in their effect on behavior. FR performance between reinforcers typically consists of a *post-reinforcement pause* (also called *pre-ratio pause*, or *latency to first response*) followed by a steady stream of responses (the *ratio run*). FI performance is similar to FR performance, but the transition from pause to response often appears to be less abrupt; this pattern is called the FI *scallop*. Responses in VR and VI (and RR and RI) schedules are typically

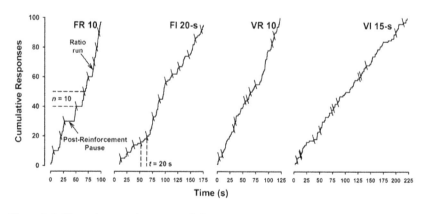

Figure 5.6. Illustrative cumulative records for FR 10, FI 20-s, VR 10, and VI 15-s.

more evenly distributed across the inter-reinforcer interval than in FR and FI performance, but VR schedules yield a higher *B* (steeper cumulative record) than VI schedules.

Schedule control is the systematic change in the pattern of response as a function of the schedule of reinforcement. A particularly strong demonstration of schedule control is the change in operant performance that results from changing only the schedule of reinforcement while keeping all else, including the rate of reinforcement (*r*), equal. For instance, *r* may be maintained invariant across VI and VR schedules by yoking it, setting up the interval requirements in the VI-schedule condition to the observed inter-reinforcer intervals in the VR-schedule condition. *B* is higher in VR than in yoked-VI schedules, indicating that schedule control is expressed as faster-responding in VR than in VI schedules (Catania, Matthews, Silverman, and Yohalem, 1977). This difference in *B* across ratio and interval schedules has motivated much theorizing on schedule control (e.g., Peele, Casey, & Silberberg, 1984).

VI and RI schedules are prevalent in operant conditioning research because, (a) unlike fixed schedules, they yield relatively steady and continuous streams of response (Figure 5.6, rightmost record), and, (b) unlike ratio schedules, interval schedules allow experimental control over *r*. In ratio schedules $r = B/n$ (e.g., 100 resp/hour in VR 20 yields a response rate of $100 / 20 = 5$ reinf/hour), so *r* is primarily under the control of the organism. In interval schedules, the investigator has substantial control over *r*, because *r* reaches its maximum ($1/t$) even with a modest *B*. For example, consider the email example used previously: As long as you check your inbox at least once in a while, you will obtain the maximum rate of important messages. If important messages are posted, say, once per day ($t = 1$ day), whether you check your inbox every hour ($B = 24$ resp/day), every minute ($B = 1,440$ resp/day), or every second ($B = 86,400$ resp/day), it does not change the rate at which you will read important messages ($r \approx 1$ message/day).

The *feedback function* of a schedule of reinforcement is the relation between *B* and *r* in that schedule (Figure 5.7). The slope of the ratio feedback function is $1/n$; the asymptote of the interval and time feedback functions is $1/t$; $r = 0$ in extinction. Interval and time schedules differ noticeably on *r* only when *B* is very low. Feedback functions do not vary between fixed and variable schedules because, in the long run, the variability in *n* and *t* does not change the relation between *B* and *r* [e.g., on both FR 10 and VR 10 schedules, responding on average twice per minute ($B = 2$ resp/min) yields, on average, one reinforcer every five minutes ($r = 0.2$ reinf/min)].

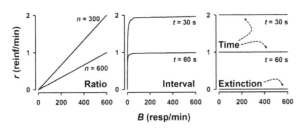

Figure 5.7. Feedback functions for ratio (left panel), interval (central panel), and time schedules, and for extinction (right panel). The functions trace the change in rate of reinforcement (*r*) with changes in rate of response (*B*).

In Box 5.13, plot two feedback functions in the same graph, one for FR 10 and another for FI 2-min. Include axis labels and units. At what rate of responding *B* do both schedules yield the same rate of reinforcement *r*?

Box 5.13

EXERCISES

1. For each of the following examples, indicate whether the learning process involved is more likely to be (purely) Pavlovian or operant. If it is Pavlovian, identify the associated stimuli; if it is operant, identify the response and outcome.

    a. Anticipating rain after seeing dark clouds
    b. Bringing out an umbrella after seeing dark clouds
    c. Being disgusted by a photograph of rotten food
    d. Covering your eyes during a horror movie

2. Paying pregnant women to stop smoking reduces their rate of smoking (Higgins et al., 2012). An investigator wants to determine whether this effect is due to operant learning. Describe the appropriate design for this study, including a control condition. Assume that rates of smoking are estimated weekly through breath carbon monoxide. What result would demonstrate operant learning in the reduction of smoking?

3. Identify the S^D, response, and outcome in each of the following examples of operant conditioning:

    a. A dog sits when its trainer gives an instruction, because treats are contingent to sitting
    b. A cat escapes a box by pulling a rope
    c. A hamster navigates a maze efficiently, at the end of which it is petted by its owner
    d. A rat traverses a shuttle-box as soon as a shock-signaling light turns on

4. Classify each of the examples in Question 3 according to the matrix in Figure 5.4. Indicate, for each example, whether the outcome is appetitive or aversive.

5. What schedule of positive reinforcement shown in Figure 5.5 best models each of the following situations? Briefly explain why.

    a. Fishing
    b. Walking home from school
    c. Auditioning for a part in a movie
    d. Studying for a weekly quiz
    e. Checking your Facebook news feed to read interesting posts

6. Two cumulative records of lever-pressing for food were obtained for the same rat (Figure 5.8). Each record (A and B) was obtained from a different simple schedule of reinforcement (FR, FI, VR, or VI). Performance on which two schedules are most likely represented in Figure 5.8? Why? What is the average rate of response on each schedule?

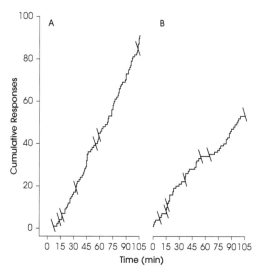

Figure 5.8. Two cumulative records obtained from performance in two different, simple schedules of reinforcement. Note that the *availability* of reinforcement in Panel B is yoked to reinforcement in Panel A.

7.   Sketch an approximate feedback function for

    a.   a negative punishment procedure, and
    b.   a DRH schedule of reinforcement.

REFERENCES

Bickel, W. K., Johnson, M. W., Koffarnus, M. N., MacKillop, J., & Murphy, J. G. (2014). The behavioral economics of substance use disorders: Reinforcement pathologies and their repair. *Annual Review of Clinical Psychology, 10*, 641–677.

Bouton, M. E., Todd, T. P., Vurbic, D., & Winterbauer, N. E. (2011). Renewal after the extinction of free operant behavior. *Learning & Behavior, 39*(1), 57–67.

Bouton, M. E., Winterbauer, N. E., & Todd, T. P. (2012). Relapse processes after the extinction of instrumental learning: Renewal, resurgence, and reacquisition. *Behavioural Processes, 90*(1), 130–141.

Brembs, B. (2003). Operant conditioning in invertebrates. *Current Opinion in Neurobiology, 13*(6), 710–717.

Catania, A. C., Matthews, T. J., Silverman, P. J., & Yohalem, R. (1977). Yoked variable—ratio and variable—interval responding in pigeons. *Journal of the Experimental Analysis of Behavior, 28*(2), 155–161.

Church, R. M. (1989). The yoked control design. In T. Archer & L. G. Nilsson (Eds.), *Aversion, avoidance, and anxiety: Perspectives on aversively motivated behavior* (pp. 403–415). Mahwah, NJ: Lawrence Erlbaum Associates.

Daniels, C. W., & Sanabria, F. (2017). Interval timing under a behavioral microscope: Dissociating motivational and timing processes in fixed-interval performance. *Learning & Behavior, 45*(1), 29–48.

Davison, M. C., & Nevin, J. A. (1999). Stimuli, reinforcers, and behavior: An integration. *Journal of the Experimental Analysis of Behavior, 71*(3), 439–482.

Dymond, S., & Roche, B. (2009). A contemporary behavioral analysis of anxiety and avoidance. *The Behavior Analyst, 32*, 7–28.

Ferster, C. B., & Skinner, B. F. (1957). *Schedules of Reinforcement*. New York, NY: Appleton-Century-Crofts.

Fleshler, M., & Hoffman, H. (1962). A progression for generating variable-interval schedules. *Journal of the Experimental Analysis of Behavior, 5*(4), 529–530.

Franks, G. J., & Lattal, K. A. (1976). Antecedent reinforcement schedule training and operant response reinstatement in rats. *Animal Learning & Behavior, 4*(4), 374–378.

Galbicka, G. (1994). Shaping in the 21st century: Moving percentile schedules into applied settings. *Journal of Applied Behavior Analysis, 27*(4), 739–760.

Henderson, J., Hurly, T. A., Bateson, M., & Healy, S. D. (2006). Timing in free-living rufous hummingbirds, Selasphorus rufus. *Current Biology, 16*(5), 512–515.

Higgins, S. T., Washio, Y., Heil, S. H., Solomon, L. J., Galeema, D. E., Higgins, T. M, et al. (2012). Financial incentives for smoking cessation among pregnant and newly postpartum women. *Preventive Medicine, 55*(S1), S33–S40.

Kearns, D. N., & Weiss, S. J. (2007). Recovery of Pavlovian sign-tracking (autoshaping) following the discontinuation of inter-trial interval food in rats. *Behavioural Processes, 75*(3), 307–311.

Levis, D. J., & Krantweiss, A. R. (2003). Working with implosive (flooding) therapy: A dynamic cognitive-behavioral exposure psychotherapy treatment approach. In W. O'Donohue, J. E. Fisher, & S. C. Hayes (Eds.), *Cognitive behavior therapy: Applying empirically supported techniques to your practice* (pp. 463–470). Hoboken, NJ: John Wiley & Sons.

Lieving, G. A., & Lattal, K. A. (2003). Recency, repeatability, and reinforcer retrenchment: An experimental analysis of resurgence. *Journal of the Experimental Analysis of Behavior, 80*(2), 217–233.

Maier, S. F., & Seligman, M. E. (1976). Learned helplessness: Theory and evidence. *Journal of Experimental Psychology: General, 105*(1), 3–46.

Peele, D. B., Casey, J., & Silberberg, A. (1984). Primacy of interresponse-time reinforcement in accounting for rate differences under variable-ratio and variable-interval schedules. *Journal of Experimental Psychology: Animal Behavior Processes, 10*(2), 149–167.

Petscher, E. S., Rey, C., & Bailey, J. S. (2009). A review of empirical support for differential reinforcement of alternative behavior. *Research in Developmental Disabilities, 30*(3), 409–425.

Pryce, C. R., Azzinnari, D., Spinelli, S., Seifritz, E., Tegethoff, M., & Meinlschmidt, G. (2011). Helplessness: A systematic translational review of theory and evidence for its relevance to understanding and treating depression. *Pharmacology & Therapeutics, 132*(3), 242–267.

Rescorla, R. A. (1997). Spontaneous recovery of instrumental discriminative responding. *Learning & Behavior, 25*(4), 485–497.

Sanabria, F., & Killeen, P. R. (2008). Evidence for impulsivity in the Spontaneously Hypertensive Rat drawn from complementary response-withholding tasks. *Behavioral and Brain Functions, 4*(1), 7.

Skinner, B. F. (1938). *The behavior of organisms: An experimental analysis.* New York, NY: Appleton-Century-Crofts.

Solomon, R. L., Kamin, L. J., & Wynne, L. C. (1953). Traumatic avoidance learning: The outcomes of several extinction procedures with dogs. *The Journal of Abnormal and Social Psychology, 48*(2), 291–302.

Stewart, J., & Badiani, A. (1993). Tolerance and sensitization to the behavioral effects of drugs. *Behavioural Pharmacology, 4*(4), 289–312.

Willcocks, A. L., & McNally, G. P. (2011). The role of context in re-acquisition of extinguished alcoholic beer-seeking. *Behavioral Neuroscience, 125*(4), 541–550.

Winterbauer, N. E., & Bouton, M. E. (2010). Mechanisms of resurgence of an extinguished instrumental behavior. *Journal of Experimental Psychology: Animal Behavior Processes, 36*(3), 343–353.

Woo, K. L., Hunt, M., Harper, D., Nelson, N. J., Daugherty, C. H., & Bell, B. D. (2009). Discrimination of flicker frequency rates in the reptile tuatara (Sphenodon). *Naturwissenschaften, 96*(3), 415–419.

Image Credits

ADVANCED CONCEPTS IN OPERANT CONDITIONING

6

COMPOUND SCHEDULES OF REINFORCEMENT

The schedules of reinforcement described in Chapter 5 model relatively simple interactions between behavior and environment. The combination of these simple schedules, known as *compound* schedules of reinforcement, may model more complex relations. The simple schedules that make up the compound schedule—its *components*—may be presented alternatively or simultaneously and may be implemented on different manipulanda (*heterogeneous* compound schedules) or on the same manipulandum (*homogeneous* compound schedules).

Stimulus control: multiple and mixed schedules. To demonstrate control of an S^D over performance, components of a compound schedule, each with a different S^D, may alternate based on the passage of time. Such a compound schedule is called a *multiple* schedule of reinforcement. For example, in multiple VI 30-s VI 60-s schedules, these two components may alternate every 10 minutes on average, with VI 30-s signaled by a high-pitch tone and VI 60-s by a low-pitch tone. Differences in B between schedules may demonstrate stimulus control, although the r on its own may acquire control of behavior. For instance, a deaf rat may detect a transition between the rich VI 30-s component and the lean VI 60-s component because of a long inter-reinforcer time. To avoid this confound, stimulus control is often demonstrated by testing the S^D for each component separately but under the same schedule (to control for r), typically extinction. Differences in extinction performance between S^D would demonstrate stimulus control (e.g., see Bouton, Todd & León, 2014).

Another method to demonstrate stimulus control is to compare performance on a multiple schedule and its corresponding *mixed* schedule of reinforcement (e.g., see Williams, Saunders & Perone, 2011). Mixed schedules are similar to multiple schedules, but the alternating components are not differentially signaled, so there is no S^D to potentially acquire control over performance. If components alternate at fixed times, changes in *B* across components of a mixed schedule may be due to the passing of time in a component. Alternatively, the difference in the temporal arrangement of reinforcement across components may gain control (*schedule* control) over behavior. For instance, if one component is an FI 30-s schedule and the other is extinction, *B* is likely to decline after a longer interval (e.g., 60 seconds) without reinforcement.

Multiple schedules of reinforcement model situations similar to those of elementary school students, whose behavior comes under the control of contextual cues (e.g., staying quiet in the classroom but frolicking in the playground). In this situation, how would you implement an analogue of a mixed schedule to determine whether behavior is indeed under stimulus control? What result would suggest that behavior is indeed under stimulus control? Write down your answer in Box 6.1.

Box 6.1

Conditioned reinforcement: chained and tandem schedules. A *primary* reinforcer (S^{r+}) reinforces a response regardless to its relation to other reinforcers. For a hungry animal, for instance, food constitutes a primary S^{r+}, because it may reinforce behavior on its own, regardless of its relation to other reinforcers. Although we have assumed so far that all S^{r+} are primary, there is another type of S^{r+}: *Conditioned* (or *secondary*) S^{r+} are those whose reinforcing properties are conditional on some association with another reinforcer. Money is a common example of a conditioned reinforcer: It is an S^{r+} for various behaviors (e.g., people work for money), but only because it allows access to other S^{r+}. In the laboratory, conditioned S^{r+} are often trained using *chained* schedules of reinforcement.

In chained schedules, components alternate when completed: Completion of the first component (the *initial link*) may be reinforced only with the transition to a second component, signaled with a different S^D, and that second component may be reinforced with the transition to a third component, signaled with another S^D, and so on. The last component in the schedule (the *terminal link*) is reinforced with a primary S^{r+}. The S^D in each link may serve as a conditioned S^{r+} that reinforces behavior in preceding links, except the initial link S^D, which has no preceding link (Williams, 1994). For example, in a chained VI 60-s FR 5 schedule of food reinforcement, an initial VI 60-s link, signaled with a continuous light, may be reinforced with access to the terminal FR 5 link, signaled with an intermittent light and reinforced with food. The intermittent light in the terminal link of the FR 5 would serve as a conditioned S^{r+} for responses in the initial VI 60-s link.

Conditioned reinforcement is demonstrated to the extent that (a) *B* increases when access to the reinforcing S^D is contingent on the response, but not when it is non-contingent, and (b) this difference is reduced when the relation between S^D and the primary reinforcer is removed. Money constitutes a conditioned S^{r+} in regards to work to the extent that reinforced work declines with (a) non-contingent money (e.g., cash gifts), and (b) a weaker relation between money and goods (e.g., inflation). If cash gifts do not reduce the amount of work, it is likely that work is maintained through means different than money. If inflation does not reduce the amount of work, it is possible that money (for whatever reason) is a primary S^{r+} itself. The demonstration of conditioned reinforcement in chained schedules also involves isolating the primary-reinforcing effects of the S^{r+} on responses that occur in non-terminal links. In a chained VI FR schedule, the S^{r+} is contingent not only on responding on the terminal FR, but also on responding on the initial VI link; without responses on the initial VI link, there would be no access to the terminal FR and no S^{r+}. To the extent that such contingency between the initial link and S^{r+} increases VI responding, food serves as a primary S^{r+} of VI responses. In general, responses on any link in a chained schedule may be a function of conditioned reinforcement (from subsequent links) and primary reinforcement (from the S^{r+}).

Selectively breaking the contingency between the terminal-link S^D and the primary S^{r+} may reveal the primary-reinforcer effects of the S^D on performance in the initial link. In the example with money, this is akin to the "inflation" scenario. In the laboratory, programming NCR or extinction in the terminal link would implement such a control condition. Selectively breaking the contingency between responding in the initial link and the S^D of the terminal link may reveal the primary-reinforcer effects of the S^{r+} on performance in the initial link. In the example with money, this is akin to the "cash gift" scenario. In the laboratory, such a control condition often takes the form of a *tandem* schedule of reinforcement.

Tandem schedules are similar to chained schedules: Completion of the initial link leads to a terminal link, which in turn leads to S^{r+}. However, in tandem schedules there is no differential S^D signaling each link, so there is no S^D reinforcing initial-link responses; only the S^{r+} maintains responding. In the money example, this is like being paid not with money, but directly with the goods you would buy with that money. All else being equal, the difference between the amount of work you would do without money and with money is the conditioned-reinforcer effect of money. In the laboratory, the difference in performance during initial links in tandem versus chained schedules is the conditioned-reinforcing effect of the terminal-link S^D in the chained schedule. A more thorough control condition would involve non-contingent alternation of the S^D in the tandem schedule, yoked to the contingent alternation in the chained schedule (Catania, Yohalem & Silverman, 1980).

Animal trainers often use conditioned reinforcement to guide behavior. This is a particularly useful tool when the primary S^{r+} (typically a treat) may not be delivered immediately after each operant—it may take too much time to deliver it, it may habituate, or it may elicit an unconditioned response (UR) that interferes with the operant, among other possible reasons. The standard training procedure involves two steps. First, the conditioned reinforcer (the equivalent of the S^D in the terminal link, e.g., a clicker sound) is paired, in a Pavlovian manner, with the primary S^{r+} (e.g., treat). Second, the operant (sitting) is reinforced with the conditioned reinforcer in the presence of an initial-link S^D (e.g., a verbal command to sit), which is followed (at least sometimes) by the primary S^{r+}. How would you transform this clicker-food training procedure into a tandem schedule? In that design, what would indicate the conditioned-reinforcer effects of the clicker on the sitting behavior? Include your answers in Box 6.2.

Box 6.2

Other compound schedules. Components of a compound schedule may also be nested within each other. In *second-order* schedules of reinforcement, completion of the first-order component is signaled by a stimulus, which is treated as a response toward the completion of the second-order component (Schindler, Panlilio & Goldberg, 2002). For instance, in a second-order FR 3 FI 1-min, completion of the FI 1-min component may result in the flash of a light; once the light flashes for a third time, S^{r+} is delivered. An important feature of second-order schedules is that the stimulus associated with completion of the first-order component (the flashing light) may acquire conditioned-reinforcer properties, by virtue of its pairing with S^{r+} (Williams, 1994). Demonstration of conditioned reinforcement in this context faces the same challenges discussed for chained schedules. Nonetheless, to the extent that such conditioned reinforcement occurs, it is expected that second-order schedules maintain more responding than a yoked first-order schedule (in the example it would be, approximately, an FI 3-min schedule).

Components of compound schedules may operate simultaneously and independently of each other. In *alternative* schedules of reinforcement, two or more simple schedules operate simultaneously, and S^{r+} is contingent on the first schedule completed. For instance, in an alternative FR 10 FI 1-min schedule, S^{r+} is delivered after either (a) 10 responses or (b) the first response once one minute has elapsed, whichever happens first. Reinforcement resets all components (i.e., the FR counter and the FI clock reset after reinforcement). *Conjoint* schedules of reinforcement are similar to alternative schedules, but the schedules always operate on the same manipulandum (i.e., conjoint schedules are always homogeneous) and reinforcement does not reset the non-completed schedule. In a conjoint FR 10 FI 1-min schedule, S^{r+} is delivered every tenth response without resetting the one-minute clock of the FI, and is also delivered for one response every minute without resetting the FR counter. *Conjunctive* schedules of reinforcement are also similar to alternative schedules, but S^{r+} is contingent on completing all components. In a conjunctive FR 10 FI 1-min schedule, S^{r+} is delivered after 10 responses, as long as one of them is emitted one minute after the last S^{r+} delivery.

CHOICE BEHAVIOR

Concurrent schedules. In natural environments, multiple independent resources are available, and the exploitation of each resource often entails ignoring other resources. Pollen, for instance, is produced independently in separate patches of flowers; for a bee, foraging for pollen in a patch of flowers located east of the hive means not foraging in another patch of flowers located west of the hive. Concurrent schedules of reinforcement model this aspect of natural environments. In these compound schedules, two or more schedules operate simultaneously and independently of each other (often times they are referred to as *independent concurrent* schedules). They are similar to conjunctive schedules, but each component operates on a separate manipulandum (i.e., concurrent schedules are heterogeneous; see, however, the *Findley procedure* in this chapter).

Concurrent schedules model choice situations: The bee has to choose how to allocate its behavior between different patches of flowers. In particular, concurrent VI-VI schedules have been extensively used in the laboratory to study choice behavior. The use of VI components in these schedules affords experimental control over a key independent variable: the *relative rate of reinforcement*, which is the ratio of reinforcers obtained from each component of the concurrent schedule over a fixed period of time (r_1/r_2). The effect of r_1/r_2 is measured on the *relative rate of responding* (B_1/B_2), which is the ratio of responses allocated to each VI component over a fixed period of time; B_1/B_2 is the main dependent variable in the study of choice. In concurrent VI VI schedules, r_1/r_2 depends primarily on the interval requirements (t_1 and t_2, programmed by the experimenter), and substantially less so on B_1/B_2 (emitted by the organism). This invariance allows for experimental control over r_1/r_2 and is evident in the feedback functions of B_1/B_2 (Figure 6.1). These functions are akin to those in Figure 5.7 (in Chapter 5), but they use relative—instead of absolute—measures of response and reinforcement. Only when response allocation is extreme (very low or very high B_1/B_2), r_1/r_2 diverges from t_2/t_1.

Concurrent schedules other than VI VI do not provide the level of control over r_1/r_2 shown in Figure 6.1. For instance, because of the linear relation between r and B in simple ratio schedules (Figure 5.7), there is also a linear relation between r_1/r_2 and B_1/B_2 in independent concurrent ratio schedules. Nonetheless, *dependent* (or *non-independent*) concurrent ratio schedules may approximate the feedback function of Figure 8 (Stubbs & Pliskoff, 1969). In these schedules, only one un-signaled and randomly-selected component is implemented after each reinforcer; r_1/r_2 reflect, in part, the relative frequency with which components are implemented.

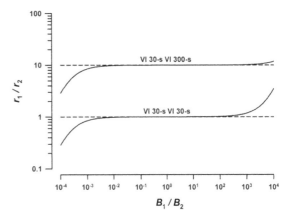

Figure 6.1. Feedback function, in a log-log plot, for concurrent VI 30-s VI 30-s ($t_2/t_1 = 1$) and concurrent VI 30-s VI 300-s ($t_2/t_1 = 10$); t_2/t_1 is indicated by dashed lines. The functions trace the change in relative rate of reinforcement (r_1/r_2) with relative rate of responding (B_1/B_2). Over a broad range of B_1/B_2 (roughly from 1/1000 to 1000), $r_1/r_2 \approx t_2/t_1$.

To contrast the level of control over r_1/r_2 in concurrent VI VI and concurrent VR VR schedules, use Box 6.3 to draw the feedback function, in a linear-linear or log-log plot, of a concurrent VR 5 VR 5 schedule and a concurrent VR 10 VR 5 schedule, similar to Figure 6.1 (i.e., plot r_1/r_2 as a function of B_1/B_2). Keep in mind that for any ratio schedule, $r = B/n$.

In concurrent VI VI schedules, the organism chooses when to switch between components. The cost of switching is an important variable, typically implemented as a short *changeover delay*, or COD. The COD is a short interval (typically shorter than five seconds) that starts with either the last response on the switch-from component or the first response on the switch-to component, during which the switched-to component is ineffective. When modeling foraging behavior, such as in the example of bees seeking pollen, the COD represents the time it takes to travel between patches of resources (Dow & Lea, 1987).

Box 6.3

Findley (1958) developed an alternative implementation of concurrent schedules that facilitates strict experimental control over the COD and other switching contingencies. Whereas the components of concurrent schedules are typically implemented in separate manipulanda, the *Findley procedure* arranges all components in the *main* manipulandum, each signaled by a different S^D. Switching between components in the main manipulandum of the Findley procedure requires completing a schedule in the *changeover* manipulandum. For example, to implement a 5-s COD, an FI 5-s may be scheduled in the changeover manipulandum.

The matching law. Concurrent VI VI performance, regardless of its implementation (independently or dependently, two manipulanda or Findley procedure), regularly shows that B_1/B_2 is a power function of r_1/r_2,

$$\frac{B_1}{B_2} = b\left(\frac{r_1}{r_2}\right)^s.$$

(6.1)

This equation is the *generalized matching law* (Baum, 1974). It may be also expressed in terms of the proportion of behavior allocated to each alternative,

$$\frac{B_1}{B_1+B_2} = \frac{b(r_1)^s}{b(r_1)^s + (r_2)^s}.$$

(6.1A)

Both equations are mathematically equivalent: Whether Equation 6.1 is true or false, so is Equation 6.1A. They are simply two different ways of expressing the same relation between a set of variables.

Strict matching—the simple identity between B_1/B_2 and r_1/r_2—is obtained when $b = s = 1$. In plain English, strict matching means that the allocation of behavior across components matches the distribution of obtained S^{r+} across components. A log-log plot relating B_1/B_2 to r_1/r_2 linearizes Equation 1, and strict matching appears as an identity line (Figure 6.2).

What allocation of behavior (B_1/B_2) does strict matching predict for concurrent VR VR schedules? Keep in mind that this schedule models situations akin to having two slot machines, each paying with a probability of $1/n$; if you knew the pay rate of each machine, how would you allocate your behavior between them? Also, recall the linear relation between r and B (i.e., $r = B/n$). Answer these questions in Box 6.4.

Box 6.4

Although the experimenter programs r_1/r_2, that does not mean that all the relevant outcomes that control choice are only r_1 and r_2. For instance, in a concurrent VI 30-s VI 60-s schedule of food reinforcement, r_1 should be about twice r_2, so strict matching predicts that the organism would allocate twice as many responses on the VI 30-s component than on the VI 60-s component. That assumes that the *only* outcome of responding to one component or the other is the food it delivers—the programmed S^{r+}. It is likely, however, that such assumption is inaccurate: When responding on the VI 30-s component, for example, the organism may be in a different location, contacting a different manipulandum than when responding on the VI 60-s component. If the appetitive and aversive properties of those extraneous outcomes were known, they could be incorporated into the computation of r_1 and r_2. To the extent that those properties have a multiplicative effect on r_1 and r_2, and are the same across components, they cancel out. If these properties are not the same, a single parameter may capture the ratio of their multiplicative effects. Parameter b in Equation 6.1 is that ratio, which reflects differences in appetitive and aversive properties of the components of the concurrent schedule that do not involve the S^{r+}. Because b is not known, it is estimated from performance, and it is expressed as *choice bias*: If $b > 1$, component 1 is chosen more than expected from strict matching; if $b < 1$, component 2 is chosen more than expected from strict matching. In a matching plot, choice bias appears as B_1/B_2 when $r_1/r_2 = 1$ (Figure 6.2, dashed lines).

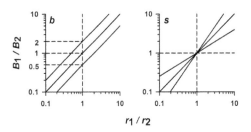

Figure 6.2. Traces of the matching law (Equation 6.1). Left panel: $s = 1.0$ and $b = 0.5$ (bottom), 1.0 (middle: identity line), and 2.0 (top). Right panel: $b = 1.0$ and $s = 0.6$ (flatter), 1.0 (diagonal: identity line), and 1.4 (steeper). Note that these plots are similar to the feedback function of Figure 6.1, but with the axes flipped.

Sensitivity of behavior allocation to the distribution of S^{r+} is somewhat variable. Under most circumstances, animals show a tendency to *undermatch*, that is, to allocate their behavior more evenly across components than expected from strict matching (Wearden & Burgess, 1982). For example, in a concurrent VI 30-s VI 60-s schedule, an undermatching animal would spend less than twice as many responses on the VI 30-s component than on the VI 60-s component (i.e., $B_1/B_2 < 2$). This tendency is exacerbated by absent CODs (Shull & Pliskoff, 1967). However, when the cost of switching between components is very high, *overmatching* is sometimes observed (Aparicio, 2001). In the previous example, an overmatching animal would spend more than twice as many responses on the VI 30-s component than on the VI 60-s component (i.e., $B_1/B_2 > 2$). In Equation 6.1, s reflects such sensitivity to the distribution of S^{r+} across alternatives: If $s < 1$, B_1/B_2 changes slower with r_1/r_2 than expected from strict matching (undermatching); if $s > 1$, B_1/B_2 changes faster with r_1/r_2 than expected from strict matching (overmatching). In a matching plot, choice sensitivity appears as the slope of the function (Figure 6.2), with flatter functions indicating undermatching and steeper functions indicating overmatching. In the most extreme case of undermatching, where $s = 0$, choice is not sensitive at all to r_1/r_2, which would be represented as a flat horizontal line.

Components of concurrent VI VI schedules may vary not only on r, but also on various other dimensions of the S^{r+}: its amount, quality, delay, etc. All else being equal, B_1/B_2 increases with larger, better, more immediate, and, in general, more efficacious S^{r+} in component 1 (see Bron, Sumpter, Foster, & Temple, 2003). It thus appears that a common hypothetical factor among these dimensions, the *value* of each component, governs B_1/B_2. A more valuable component attracts more behavior because it delivers more frequent, larger, better, or more immediate S^{r+}. Therefore, when qualitatively different S^{r+} (e.g., sweetened condensed milk and dry food) are programmed on concurrent VI VI schedules, choice bias in one direction or the other may provide an objective measure of relative value of the S^{r+}. Although such a feature of concurrent VI VI schedules has had important implications for behavioral economics and foraging theory (Herrnstein, 1997), more recent developments, discussed in the Behavioral Economics section of this chapter, undermine a simple interpretation of choice bias as relative value.

The matching law has important implications even for simple schedules of reinforcement. Behavior in a simple schedule may be thought of as a choice between the operant (B_1) and every other behavior that is inconsistent with the operant (B_0). Because all behavior falls into one of these two categories, their sum constitutes the totality of behavior, and that totality is constant: $B_1 + B_0 = k$. If it is assumed that the schedule reinforces the operant at a rate r_1, and an implicit schedule reinforces all other behavior at rate r_0, strict matching predicts that

$$B_1 = \frac{kr_1}{r_1 + r_0}.$$

(6.2)

Equation 6.2, which may be easily derived from Equation 6.1A assuming $b = s = 1$ and $B_1 + B_0 = k$, is the *quantitative law of effect* (Herrnstein, 1970). Assuming a constant implicit rate of reinforcement (r_0), it predicts that the response rate on a simple schedule (B_1) increases as a negatively accelerated function of rate of reinforcement (r_1) toward an asymptote of k (cf. Figure 2.7C in Chapter 2). Figure 2.6 in Chapter 2 shows fits of the quantitative law of effect on VI performance in three strains of rat. Based on that figure, indicate in Box 6.5 the most likely value of k for SHR and WIS rats.

Box 6.5

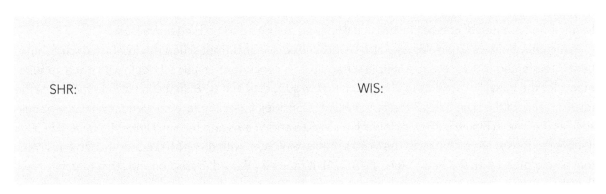

SHR: WIS:

The quantitative law of effect provides key insights into the mechanisms of reinforcement. It indicates, for instance, that reinforcement depends not only on S^{r+} and the schedule on which it is programmed, but also on other stimuli present during conditioning. Just like habituated, sensitized, and Pavlovian-conditioned behavior, operant behavior does not occur in a void: Stimuli in the environment, other than the manipulandum and the S^{r+}, constitute the context of operant behavior. These stimuli interfere with operant behavior by attracting behavior away from the schedule of reinforcement. From this perspective, reinforcement operates by guiding the allocation of limited resources—time or responses—among alternatives.

Choosing between schedules: concurrent-chains schedules. Although B_1/B_2 appears to index the preference between components of a concurrent schedule, schedule control exerted by each component is likely to interfere with the expression of preference. For example, in a concurrent VR 100 FI 30-s schedule, an organism is likely to make most responses on the VR schedule and only visit the FI schedule around 30 s since the last reinforcer

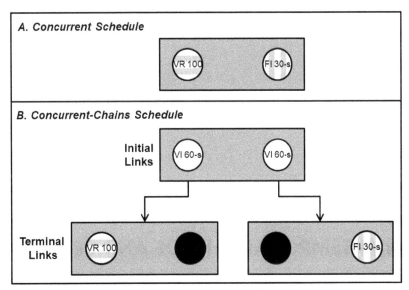

Figure 6.3. **A.** An illustrative concurrent schedule of reinforcement. **B.** An illustrative concurrent-chains schedule.

(Sanabria, Thrailkill, & Killeen, 2009). This pattern may emerge because VR schedules maintain a steady and high B, whereas FI responses cluster around the interval requirement. This pattern reveals a competition for schedule control, not a competition for preference.

Concurrent-chains schedules of reinforcement are often used to study choice between simple schedules (Davison, 1987). Just like concurrent schedules involve the concurrent availability of two simple schedules, concurrent-chains schedules involve the concurrent availability of the initial link of each of two chained schedules (Figure 6.3). Recall that, in chained schedules, the initial link does not yield a primary reinforcer; instead, it yields access to another simple schedule—the terminal link. In concurrent-chains schedules, a distinct S^D signals each terminal link, distinguishing it not only from its initial link, but also from other terminal links. Whereas initial links are available concurrently, terminal links are not: Once a terminal link is entered, non-reinforced initial links are paused and no longer available.

Concurrent-chains schedules may also be described as concurrent schedules in which each component is reinforced with access to a simple schedule. In a concurrent-chains schedule with equal requirements for the initial link schedules, the matching law suggests that B_1/B_2 in the initial links measures the relative value of the schedules in the terminal link. Consider, for example, a concurrent-chains schedule such as the one in Figure 6.3B, with initial links VI 60-s and VI 60-s and terminal links VR 100 and FI 30-s. If more responses are allocated to the VI 60-s that is reinforced with the VR 100 rather than to the VI 60-s that is reinforced with the FI 30-s (i.e., $B_1/B_2 > 1$), it may be inferred, based on the strict matching law, that the VR 100 schedule is more valuable than the FI 30-s schedule.

Concurrent-chains schedules of reinforcement are widely applied to assess complex choice. For instance, risk preference may be assessed using concurrent-chains schedules. How would you program a concurrent-chains schedule of reinforcement to assess the preference between an outcome that is unpredictable and one that is predictable? Draw your answer as a diagram similar to Figure 6.3B.

Box 6.6

INTERTEMPORAL CHOICE AND SELF-CONTROL

A particularly interesting complex choice is the *intertemporal choice* between small but immediate (*smaller-sooner*) S^{r+} and delayed but large (*larger-later*) S^{r+}. Choosing the smaller-sooner S^{r+} is often deemed impulsive, whereas choosing the larger-later S^{r+} is deemed self-controlled (Madden & Bickel, 2010). For someone battling alcoholism, choosing between drinking to inebriation now and the healthy but delayed outcome of sobriety is an intertemporal choice. Intertemporal choice is also critical to assess how the value of an S^{r+} declines as a function of the delay to its delivery, a process known as *delay discounting*. Most hungry animals prefer food sooner rather than later, just as most humans prefer $100 now rather than in a week. This indicates that food and money (and, in fact, most S^{r+}) lose value as they are postponed.

Assessment of delay discounting. Similar to other complex choice situations, concurrent-chains schedules may model intertemporal choice. Oliveira, Green and Myerson (2014), for instance, presented pigeons with a concurrent-chains schedule with initial links VI 30-s VI 30-s and terminal links of fixed-time (FT) 0.3-s, reinforced with a variable but small number of food pellets (smaller-sooner alternative), and FT 20-s reinforced with 16 pellets

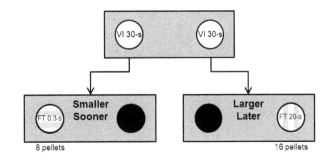

Figure 6.4. Illustrative intertemporal choice, represented as a concurrent-chains schedule. The specific parameters are from Oliveira, et al. (2014). The smaller-sooner terminal link yielded a variable number of pellets, but always fewer than 16, (e.g., eight pellets).

(larger-later alternative; Figure 6.4). By varying the size of the smaller-sooner S^{r+}, Oliveira et al. determined the immediate value of the larger-later S^{r+}. More specifically, this *adjusted-amount procedure* involved varying the size of the smaller-sooner S^{r+} depending on the relative rate of response on its corresponding initial link (B_{SS}/B_{LL}): It decreased when B_{SS}/B_{LL} exceeded a threshold (1.2) and increased when it fell below a lower threshold (0.8). This method stabilized B_{SS}/B_{LL} at about 1.0, when the pigeon was equally likely to choose the smaller-sooner and the larger-later alternatives. This indifference between a smaller-sooner and a larger-later S^{r+} may be represented as a point in an empirical function relating delay to the larger-later S^{r+} and size of the smaller-sooner S^{r+}. Figure 6.5 shows the *indifference points* for the delayed 16-pellet outcome at five different delays for one pigeon in the Oliveira et al. study. The rightmost point in Figure 6.5 shows that this pigeon was indifferent between 16 pellets delayed by 20 seconds and one pellet delayed by 0.3 seconds. Based on the matching law, it may be

inferred that, for this particular pigeon, 16 pellets delayed by 20 seconds is worth one pellet now; in other words, the 16 pellets lost about 94 percent of their value because they were delayed by 20 seconds. The rest of the indifferent points in Figure 6.5 show a more detailed trajectory of the loss of value as a function of delay: 25 percent after just one second, 50 percent after three seconds, and so on.

There are multiple methods to determine the indifference points that constitute an empirical delay discounting function. Initial links, in fact, are rarely VI schedules; they are more often continuous reinforcement (CRF) schedules, ensuring exposure to both terminal links through forced-choice trials, in which animals only have access to one initial link (Mazur, 1987). Aside from the adjusting-amount procedure, adjusting-delay procedures have been implemented, in which the delay to the smaller-sooner S^{r+} varies with B_{SS}/B_{LL} (Mazur, 1987). In humans, choice is typically assessed using hypothetical rewards, such as money, and asking questions such as "Would you prefer $20,000 in a year or $15,000 now?" Human indifference points are estimated using a broad range of adjusting and non-adjusting methods (for a review, see Hamilton, Mitchell, Wing, Balodis, Bickel, Fillmore, et al., 2015).

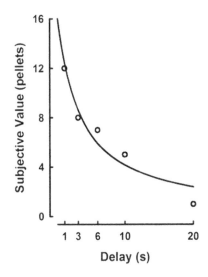

Figure 6.5. Subjective value of 16 pellets for a pigeon, as a function of delay. The subjective value is the magnitude of the immediate S^{r+} that is chosen about as often as the delayed 16 pellets. The continuous curve is a fitted hyperbolic discount function (see Equation 6.4). Based on one subject (P38) from Oliveira et al. (2014).

Exponential discounting function. As illustrated in Figure 6.5, delay discounting functions are typically negatively accelerated with a negative slope and an asymptote of zero (cf. Figure 2.7D in Chapter 2). This means that, as a reinforcer becomes more delayed, its value approaches zero, which may result from a decline in value at a constant rate. For example, if that rate was 50 percent per second for a pigeon, it would mean that eight pellets, if delayed by one second, are worth only four pellets now (i.e., the pigeon would be indifferent between four pellets now and eight pellets in one second); if delayed by two seconds they are worth two pellets now; if delayed by three seconds they are worth one pellet now, etc. This relation between delay and value may be expressed more generally as a continuous *exponential discounting function,*

$$V(S^{r+},\ D) = V(S^{r+},\ 0)e^{-\lambda D},$$

(6.3)

where $V(S^{r+}, D)$ is the value of S^{r+} after delay D, $V(S^{r+}, 0)$ is the value of that same S^{r+} if it is available immediately ($D = 0$), and λ is the discounting rate, where a larger λ means a steeper discounting function. A discounting rate of 50 percent per second would correspond to $\lambda = -\ln(.5) = 0.693$ s^{-1}.

Time consistency, preference reversal, and commitment. The exponential discounting function is typically used by financial institutions and other rational economic agents to discount the value of delayed goods (e.g., the payments you make, with interest, for money borrowed from your bank). Exponential discounting is rational because it is *time consistent*: It does not change the preference between alternatives when the same delay is added to all alternatives. If you prefer an apple now over an orange tomorrow, adding 10 days to both alternatives while keeping everything else equal should not change your preference; you should still prefer an apple in 10 days over an orange in 11 days. Note that the rationality of the discounting function is not in the preference itself—there is nothing rational or irrational about your preference between apple and oranges, or between $10 now and $100 tomorrow. An individual may be very impulsive (e.g., prefer $10 now over $100 tomorrow) and yet be perfectly rational, because his choices are time consistent (e.g., also prefers $10 in 120 days over $100 in 121 days). The time consistency of exponential discounting is reflected in Figure 6.6A and 6.6B, where discount functions with the same λ do not cross each other, regardless of λ.

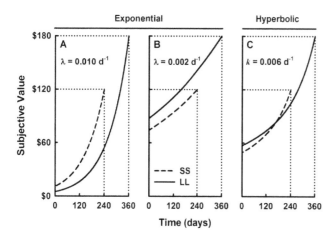

Figure 6.6. A. Illustrative exponential discounting functions of a smaller-sooner (SS = $120 in 240 d) and a larger-later (LL = $180 in 360 d), with $\lambda = 0.010$ d^{-1}. The dotted lines indicate the delay (relative to time = 0 d) and magnitude of the rewards. As time elapses, the delay to both rewards declines (e.g., at time = 240 d; the delay to SS = 0 d), and subjective value increases. **B.** Exponential discounting functions of SS and LL, but with a lower discount rate ($\lambda = 0.002$ d^{-1}). **C.** Hyperbolic discounting functions of SS and LL, with $k = 0.006$ d^{-1}. Note that hyperbolic discounting functions, unlike exponential discounting functions, cross over, indicating a preference reversal.

The choices of individual animals and humans, however, do not appear to be time consistent. Instead of declining at a constant rate over time, as Equation 6.3 would predict, value appears to decline at a faster rate with shorter delays. This divergence from exponential discounting has critical implications. Functions that decline faster at shorter delays than at longer delays may cross over, such that choosing smaller-sooner S^{r+} is more likely at shorter delays, and choosing larger-later S^{r+} is more likely at longer delays. For instance, the pigeon that chooses three pellets now over eight pellets in two seconds is likely to choose eight pellets in 62 seconds over three pellets in 60 seconds. Even a very impulsive individual who chooses $10 now over $100 tomorrow is likely to choose $100 in 121 days over $10 in 120 days. Such switch in choice when the same delay is added to two S^{r+} (60 seconds in the pigeon example, 120 days in the impulsive individual example) is known as a *preference reversal*.

Preference reversals are regularly observed when a common delay is added to two alternatives in an intertemporal choice (e.g., Krebs & Anderson, 2012). In fact, pigeons that choose a smaller-sooner over a larger-later alternative, also choose to cancel the smaller-sooner alternative if given the opportunity a few seconds earlier (Rachlin & Green, 1972). Such *commitment* to the larger-later alternative only makes sense if there is a preference reversal between the time of commitment and the time when intertemporal choice may be made.

Hyperbolic discounting function. Among the many models that account for preference reversals in intertemporal choice (e.g., van den Bos & McClure, 2013), a particularly prevalent one is the *hyperbolic discounting function* (Mazur, 1987),

$$V(S^{r+}, D) = \frac{V(S^{r+}, 0)}{1+kD}. \tag{6.4}$$

In Equation 6.4, *k* is the discounting rate; like λ, a larger *k* means a steeper discounting function. Aside from its simplicity, the hyperbolic discount function has a solid theoretical foundation because it can be derived from the matching law (Chung & Herrnstein, 1967).[1]

As shown in Figure 6.6C, two hyperbolic discounting functions, even with the same discounting rate, may cross over. According to this function, a pigeon with $k = 0.5\ s^{-1}$ would prefer five pellets now over eight pellets in two seconds, because the larger-later reinforcer is worth only $8/(1 + 0.5\ s^{-1} \times 2\ s)$ = 4 pellets. However, the same pigeon would prefer eight pellets in 62 seconds over five pellets in 60 seconds, because the former would be worth 0.25 pellets, whereas the latter would be worth about 0.16 pellets. In other words, the hyperbolic discounting function—unlike the exponential discounting function—allows for preference reversals.

Because the hyperbolic discounting function predicts preference reversals regularly observed in choice behavior, it generally fits empirical data much better than the exponential discounting function (Figure 6.5). When estimated is humans, the discounting parameter *k* appears to be associated with a host of problem behaviors related to impulsivity, such as cigarette smoking (e.g., Yoon, Higgins, Heil, Sugarbaker, Thomas, & Badger, 2007) and overeating (Weller, Cook, Avsar, & Cox, 2008). Nonetheless, it is important to mention that small variations of Equation 6.4 have been shown to improve its fit to empirical data (e.g., McKerchar, Green, Myerson, Pickford, Hill & Stout, 2009), which suggests the involvement of more parameters in the discounting of delayed value.

---

1 The rate of reinforcement, *r*, is the reciprocal of the average time between consecutive S^{r+}. So, according to Equation 6.1, keeping all else constant, B_1 (and, thus, the value of alternative 1 relative to alternative 2) is a reciprocal function of the delay to its S^{r+}.

BEHAVIORAL ECONOMICS

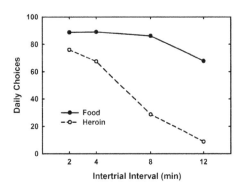

Figure 6.7. Mean number of choices of food (3 g) and heroin (0.1 mg/kg, intravenously) as a function of inter-trial interval in a baboon. Based on subject P241 in Elsmore et al. (1980).

Income-dependent choice. Concurrent VI VI schedules with identical components (e.g., VI 30-s VI 30s) appear to be useful tools for assessing the relative value of two alternatives, whether they are qualitatively different outcomes (e.g., food vs. cocaine), quantitatively different outcomes delivered at different times (i.e., inter-temporal choice), or access to different schedules of reinforcement (i.e., concurrent-chains schedules). Concurrent VI VI schedules, however, do not capture an important property of choice behavior: The allocation of choices between alternatives depends on the rate at which those choices are made. This is well demonstrated in a classic experiment by Elsmore, Fletcher, Conrad and Sodetz (1980). They allowed baboons to choose between three grams of food and 0.1 mg/kg of intravenous heroin. They found that, when choices were abundant (available every two minutes), baboons chose food and heroin about equally, but as choices became more scarce (available every 12 minutes), baboons chose food three to six times as often as heroin (Figure 6.7).

In concurrent VI VI schedules with identical components, the availability of choices can be manipulated through the interval requirement, t: Choices are more abundant when t is low (e.g., 10 seconds) than when it is high (e.g., 600 seconds). The matching law predicts that, as long as the relative rate of reinforcement is kept constant (in concurrent VI VI schedules with identical components, $r_1/r_2 \approx 1$), choice (B_1/B_2) remains constant. However, empirical research shows that choice of a larger reinforcer in concurrent VI VI schedules with identical components declines as t increases (Fantino, Squires, Delbrück, & Peterson, 1972). A similar effect is observed in concurrent-chains schedules: Choice for the preferred of two terminal links (e.g., FI 8-s relative to FI 16-s) declines as t increases in the initial link; this

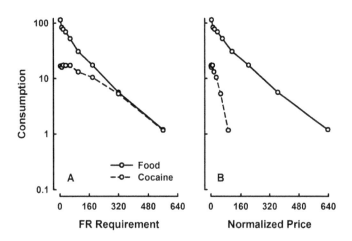

Figure 6.8. **A.** Elasticity of demand for food and cocaine (1 mg/kg, intravenously) for rats, represented as mean consumption under FR schedules with n ranging from 3 to 560, and as a normalized price (number of responses required to obtain one percent of maximal consumption). Based on Christensen et al. (2008), Experiment 1.

is known as the *initial-link effect* (Grace, Berg & Kyonka, 2006). In self-control situations, the larger-later reinforcer is more likely to be chosen if choices are scarcer (Smethells & Reilly, 2015), an effect that is consistent with preference reversal.

In economic terms, these effects indicate that the value of a reinforcer depends on the number of opportunities to obtain the reinforcer, or the *income*. Fewer choices and higher t constitute lower income. Similarly, a reduction in salary constitutes a reduction in income because there are fewer opportunities to buy goods with a lower salary. With a higher salary, we may spend as much money on non-essential goods, such as going to movies, as we do paying for essential goods, such as food and utilities. With a lower salary, however, we would probably spend less in non-essential goods than on essential goods, just as baboons spend less (in terms of choices) on heroin and more on food. The generalized matching law (Equation 6.1) does not predict income-dependent changes in choice.

Elasticity of demand. The dependency of choice on income suggests that behavior allocation alone is not an adequate measure of the intrinsic value of the reinforcer. Hursh and other investigators have suggested that the *elasticity of demand* for a good is a better measure of the value of that good (see Hursh & Silberberg, 2008; Hursh & Roma, 2016). The demand for a good is the amount of that good that the organism consumes over a period of time (e.g., in Figure 6.7, slightly below 90 heroin infusions/day, when available every two minutes). The elasticity of that demand is the slope of its decline as a function of price. In humans, price is typically instantiated in a currency, such as U.S. dollars. In non-human organisms, price is typically instantiated in number of responses required to obtain the good [i.e., as a fixed-ratio (FR) requirement, or n (Table 5.1)]. For instance, Figure 6.8 shows the average number of food pellets and cocaine infusions obtained by six rats, with the price shown as n (Panel A) and as the number of responses required to obtain one percent of maximal consumption (Panel B; Christensen, Silberberg, Hursh, Huntsberry & Riley, 2008). The latter normalized plot shows more clearly that the demand for cocaine in these rats is more elastic (declines faster with price) than the demand for food. That is, from this perspective, food is more valuable than cocaine for these rats.

In Box 6.7, identify two S^{r+} (1 and 2) and draw a demand curve for each in a single plot. The demand of S^{r+} 1 should be more elastic than the demand for S^{r+} 2. Express price in terms of FR requirement (n), and demand in terms of S^{r+} obtained.

Box 6.7

S^{r+} 1 (more elastic demand): _____

S^{r+} 2 (less elastic demand): _____

It is important to note that income and price are closely related concepts: As price increases for all S^{r+}, the number of opportunities to obtain any S^{r+} (income) declines. For example, if you have $100 and the price of bananas and avocados is $1 and $2, respectively, you can buy up to 100 bananas (zero avocados) or up to 50 avocados (zero bananas). If your income is halved (from $100 to $50) or the price of bananas and avocados is doubled, the result is the same to you: You can only buy up to 50 bananas (zero avocados) or up to 25 avocados (zero bananas). So, reducing the number of opportunities for food and heroin for the baboons in Figure 6.7 was the same as increasing the price of both S^{r+}.

Economic substitutes and complements. A key variable that modulates the elasticity of demand for a good is the availability of *substitute* and *complementary* goods. The substitutability and complementarity of two goods is defined by the effect of a change of price in one good on the demand for the other good. When two goods are economic substitutes, the increase in price in one of them yields an increase in demand for the other. For example, for many people Coke and Pepsi are economic substitutes, such that if the price of Coke is raised, the demand for Pepsi increases. When two goods are economic complements, the increase in price in one of the them yields a decrease in demand for the other. For animals, if the price of water increases, the demand for salty foods decreases.

Note that all the predictions of the matching law were described in terms of the choice between perfectly substitutable goods: The S^{r+} in most tests of the matching law is identical in both alternatives. Although the matching law makes no mention of the substitutability of the S^{r+} in each alternative, Rachlin, Kagel and Battalio (1980) suggest that the sensitivity parameter s in Equation 6.1 is related to that substitutability. In particular, they suggest that s approaches 1 with substitutable alternatives and declines toward negative infinity with complementary alternatives.

MECHANISMS OF REINFORCEMENT

Behavioral economics provides important insights into the mechanisms that govern operant reinforcement. In general terms, it suggests that reinforcement reflects an increase in the allocation of behavior to one alternative course of action among many concurrently available. That allocation appears to depend on the value of the outcome it yields, the price of that outcome, and the price of available substitute and complementary goods. These are not, however, the only mechanisms at play during conditioning. In this last section, we will review a few other mechanisms.

Induction. Although operant reinforcement is defined by the increase in the rate of the response that produces the S^{r+}, reinforcement also increases behavior other than the operant. These non-target behaviors are not reinforced; they are *induced* (Segal, 1972). Two examples of induced (or *adjunctive*) behavior are so-called *superstitious* behavior (Skinner, 1948; Staddon & Simmelhag, 1971) and *schedule-induced polydipsia* (Falk, 1961; Moreno & Flores, 2012). Both behaviors appear when food is delivered periodically and non-contingently (i.e., on an FT schedule). Superstitious behaviors were first reported as idiosyncratic and repetitive movements in pigeons, such as turning and head thrusting (Skinner, 1948). These behaviors increase in frequency with food delivery, but food delivery is not contingent on them. A more systematic examination revealed that these idiosyncrasies happen soon after each food delivery; behavior immediately before feeding is more stereotyped and directed to the source of food (Staddon & Simmelhag, 1971). Under these conditions, if water is made available, rodents typically substitute the idiosyncratic adjunctive behavior with excessive bouts of drinking, a behavior known as polydipsia (e.g., see Íbias, Pellón, & Sanabria, 2015). Some theories suggest, for instance, that the temporal proximity between behavior and the appetitive stimulus governs adjunctive and reinforced behavior (Killeen & Pellón, 2013; Skinner, 1948). Although these single-mechanism theories often blur the distinction between induction and reinforcement, the distinction between procedure (reinforcement) and process (temporal proximity) is critical to avoid confusion.

Instinctive drift. Just like unconditional effects are nested within Pavlovian conditioning (Chapter 4), unconditional effects and Pavlovian learning are nested within operant conditioning. In fact, an important source of induced behavior is the Pavlovian association between S^D and S^{r+}. Although mediated by the operant, the S^D and S^{r+} are paired and an association between them may be learned, which would be expressed as anticipatory responding to the S^{r+} in the presence of the S^D. These anticipatory responses are particularly visible when they interfere with the operant. Breland and Breland (1961) provide a classic example of such interference in what they termed *instinctive drift*. In one case of instinctive drift, a raccoon was trained to pick up a coin and deposit it in a box. The operant (depositing the coin in the box) was reinforced with food. To the bewilderment of the investigators, soon after learning to perform this simple action, the raccoon engaged in seemingly bizarre behavior: Instead of simply dropping the coin, raccoons spent a long time rubbing the coin against the inside of the container and pulling it back out. One explanation for this "misbehavior" is that the coin serves as a Pavlovian CS for the food US, eliciting the feeding-related behavior to the coins, just as a lit-key paired with food elicits pecking during sign tracking (Chapter 4). Unlike sign tracking, however, the feeding-related behavior elicited by the coins (rubbing) is inconsistent with the operant (depositing) and interferes with it.

Pavlovian-instrumental transfer. Pavlovian learning may not only interfere with operant conditioning; it may also facilitate it. The presentation during operant food reinforcement of a previously-trained Pavlovian CS that predicts a food US, further elevates the rate of response (*B*). This effect is known as *Pavlovian-instrumental transfer* (Holmes, Marchand, & Coutureau, 2010). This effect suggests that *B* is not only governed by the response-reinforcer contingency (as suggested by behavioral economics), but also by the concurrent S^D-reinforcer contingency.

EXERCISES

1. In a concurrent VI t_1 VI t_2 schedule of reinforcement, a rat responds at rate B_1 on the VI t_1 component and at rate B_2 on the VI t_2 component. Using the strict matching law, complete the missing information in each of the following scenarios.

    a. $t_1 = 1$ min $t_2 = 2$ min $B_1 = 10$ resp/min $B_2 = $ _____
    b. $t_1 = 60$ s $t_2 = $ _____ $B_1 = 10$ resp/min $B_2 = 20$ resp/min
    c. $t_1 = 15$ s $t_2 = 45$ s $B_1 = $ _____ $B_1 + B_2 = 12$ resp/min

2. The following scenarios describe the data of a monkey on a concurrent VI VI schedule. For each scenario, indicate which of the following is most likely true: $b < 1$, $b > 1$, $s < 1$, $s > 1$.

    a. When $r_1/r_2 = 0.10$, $B_1/B_2 = 0.32$; when $r_1/r_2 = 9.00$, $B_1/B_2 = 3.00$
    b. When $r_1/r_2 = 0.10$, $B_1/B_2 = 0.32$; when $r_1/r_2 = 9.00$, $B_1/B_2 = 19.00$

3. Bourret & Vollmer (2003) showed that in basketball players, the choice between shooting two-pointers and three-pointers is governed by the matching law. You are planning on replicating their study by tracking the choices (B_1/B_2) of a single professional player over the course of five games.

    a. List the relevant variables that you would record for each game to demonstrate the matching law in the choice between shooting two-pointers and three-pointers. Be very specific.

b. Based on these variables, use hypothetical data to draw a graph that would show a slight bias toward shooting two-pointers. You should have five data points, one per game.

4. Celeste is a six-year old child who can spend any proportion of 30 minutes between two concurrently available caretakers, Andrew and Betsy, in each of two days. The table that follows shows how much time Andrew and Betsy played with Celeste, and how much time Celeste spent with Andrew and Betsy. Complete the table, assuming that (a) the time spent with Andrew and the time spent with Betsy adds to 30 minutes, (b) playing with a caretaker reinforces spending time with that caretaker, and (c) there is slight undermatching.

DAY	TIME PLAYING WITH ANDREW (MIN)	TIME PLAYING WITH BETSY (MIN)	TIME SPENT WITH ANDREW (MIN)	TIME SPENT WITH BETSY (MIN)
Monday	6	3		
Tuesday			5	25

5. In a concurrent-chains schedule of reinforcement, a pigeon responds at rate B_1 and B_2 on the initial links components. Both initial links components are identical VI t schedules; the terminal links are FI 15-s and FI 30-s. To illustrate the initial-links effect, draw a hypothetical function tracking B_1/B_2 as a function of t.

6. Draw two hyperbolic delay discounting functions of $100, one for an individual with a delay discounting rate of $k = 0.1$ days^{-1}, and another with a delay discounting rate of $k = 0.01$ days^{-1}. Each function should have three data points (include value at delay = 0 days, but do not count it as a data point).

7. A dog emits more responses for getting pet than for a treat on FR 1 schedules, but emits more responses for a treat than for getting pet on FR 100 schedules. Using these data, draw one graph with two reasonable demand curves, one for getting pet and one for treats. From a behavioral-economic perspective, which of these two goods is more valuable for the dog?

8. A monkey has access to three buttons: one to obtain peanuts, one to obtain grapes, and one to obtain 1 ml of water. To obtain a reward, the monkey must press the corresponding button five times. Design a study to test your hypothesis that grapes and water are economic substitutes. Indicate what results would support your hypothesis.

9. In a chained VI 3-min FI 10-s schedule of reinforcement, you are concerned that the terminal-link S^D is inducing instinctive drift. What control condition would allow you to test this hypothesis? What results would support it?

REFERENCES

Aparicio, C. F. (2001). Overmatching in rats: The barrier choice paradigm. *Journal of the Experimental Analysis of Behavior, 75*, 93–106.

Baum, W. M. (1974). On two types of deviation from the matching law: Bias and undermatching. *Journal of the Experimental Analysis of Behavior, 22*(1), 231–242.

Bourret, J. & Vollmer, T. R. (2003). Basketball and the matching law. *Behavioral Technology Today, 3*, 2–6.

Bouton, M. E., Todd, T. P., & León, S. P. (2014). Contextual control of discriminated operant behavior. *Journal of Experimental Psychology: Animal Learning and Cognition, 40*(1), 92–105.

Breland, K., & Breland, M. (1961). The misbehavior of organisms. *American Psychologist, 16*, 681–684.

Bron, A., Sumpter, C. E., Foster, T. M., & Temple, W. (2003). Contingency discriminability, matching, and bias in the concurrent-schedule responding of possums (Trichosurus vulpecula). *Journal of the Experimental Analysis of Behavior, 79*(3), 289–306.

Catania, A. C., Matthews, T. J., Silverman, P. J., & Yohalem, R. (1977). Yoked variable-ratio and variable-interval responding in pigeons. *Journal of the Experimental Analysis of Behavior, 28*(2), 155–161.

Catania, A. C., Yohalem, R., & Silverman, P. J. (1980). Contingency and stimulus change in chained schedules of reinforcement. *Journal of the Experimental Analysis of Behavior, 33*, 213–219.

Christensen, C. J., Silberberg, A., Hursh, S. R., Huntsberry, M. E., & Riley, A. L. (2008). Essential value of cocaine and food in rats: Tests of the exponential model of demand. *Psychopharmacology, 198*, 221–229.

Chung, S. H., & Herrnstein, R. J. (1967). Choice and delay of reinforcement. *Journal of the Experimental Analysis of Behavior, 10*(1), 67–74.

Davison, M. C. (1987). The analysis of concurrent-chain performance. In M. L. Commons, J. E. Mazur, J. A. Nevin, & H. Rachlin (Eds.), *The effect of delay and of intervening events on reinforcement value. Quantitative analyses of behavior* (Vol. 5, pp. 225–241). Hillsdale, NJ: Lawrence Erlbaum Associates.

Dow, S. M., & Lea, S. E. (1987). Foraging in a changing environment: Simulations in the operant laboratory. In M. L. Commons, A. Kacelnik, & S. J. Shettleworth (Eds.), *Quantitative analyses of behavior: Foraging* (Vol. 6, pp. 89–113). Hillsdale, NJ: Lawrence Erlbaum Associates.

Elsmore, T. F., Fletcher, G. V., Conrad, D. G., & Sodetz, F. J. (1980). Reduction in heroin intake in baboons by an economic constraint. *Pharmacology, Biochemistry & Behavior, 13*(5), 729–73.

Falk, J. L. (1961). Production of polydipsia in normal rats by an intermittent food schedule. *Science, 133*(3447), 195–196.

Fantino, E., Squires, N., Delbrück, N., & Peterson, C. (1972). Choice behavior and the accessibility of the reinforcer. *Journal of the Experimental Analysis of Behavior, 18*(1), 35–42.

Findley, J. D. (1958). Preference and switching under concurrent scheduling. *Journal of the Experimental Analysis of Behavior, 1*(2), 123–144.

Grace, R. C., Berg, M. E., & Kyonka, E. G. E. (2006). Choice and timing in concurrent chains: Effects of initial-link duration. *Behavioural Processes, 71*, 188–200.

Hamilton, K. R., Mitchell, M. R., Wing, V. C., Balodis, I. M., Bickel, W. K., Fillmore, M., et al. (2015). Choice impulsivity: Definitions, measurement issues, and clinical implications. *Personality Disorders: Theory, Research, and Treatment, 6*(2), 182–198.

Herrnstein, R. J. (1970). On the law of effect. *Journal of the Experimental Analysis of Behavior, 13*(2), 243.

Herrnstein, R. J. (1997). *The matching law: Papers in psychology and economics.* D. I. Laibson & H. Rachlin (Eds.). Cambridge, MA: Harvard University Press.

Hodos, W. (1961). Progressive ratio as a measure of reward strength. *Science, 134*(3483), 943–944.

Holmes, N. M., Marchand, A. R., & Coutureau, E. (2010). Pavlovian to instrumental transfer: A neurobehavioural perspective. *Neuroscience & Biobehavioral Reviews, 34*(8), 1277–1295.

Hursh, S. R., & Roma, P. G. (2016). Behavioral economics and the analysis of consumption and choice. *Managerial and Decision Economics, 37*, 224–238.

Hursh, S. R., & Silberberg, A. (2008). Economic demand and essential value. *Psychological Review, 115*(1), 186–197.

Hursh, S. R., & Winger, G. (1995). Normalized demand for drugs and other reinforcers. *Journal of the Experimental Analysis of Behavior, 64*(3), 373–384.

Íbias, J., Pellón, R., & Sanabria, F. (2015). A microstructural analysis of schedule-induced polydipsia reveals incentive-induced hyperactivity in an animal model of ADHD. *Behavioural Brain Research, 278*, 417–423.

Killeen, P. R., & Pellón, R. (2013). Adjunctive behaviors are operants. *Learning & Behavior, 41*(1), 1–24.

Krebs, C. A., & Anderson, K. G. (2012). Preference reversals and effects of D-amphetamine on delay discounting in rats. *Behavioural Pharmaclogy, 23*, 228–240.

Madden, G. J., & Bickel, W. K. (Eds.) (2010). *Impulsivity: The behavioral and neurological science of discounting.* Washington, DC: American Psychological Association.

Mazur, J. E. (1987). An adjusting procedure for studying delayed reinforcement. In M. L. Commons, J. E. Mazur, J. A. Nevin, & H. Rachlin (Eds.) *Quantitative analyses of behavior: The effect of delay and of intervening events on reinforced value* (Vol. V, pp. 55–73). Hillsdale, NJ: Lawrence Erlbaum Associates.

McKerchar, T. L., Green, L., Myerson, J., Pickford, T. S., Hill, J. C., & Stout, S. S. (2009). A comparison of four models of delay discounting in humans. *Behavioral Processes, 81*, 256–159.

Moreno, M., & Flores, P. (2012). Schedule-induced polydipsia as a model of compulsive behavior: Neuropharmacological and neuroendocrine bases. *Psychopharmacology, 219*(2), 647–659.

Oliveira, L., Green, L., & Myerson, J. (2014). Pigeons' delay discounting functions established using a concurrent-chains procedure. *Journal of the Experimental Analysis of Behavior, 102*, 151–161.

Rachlin, H., & Green, L. (1972). Commitment, choice and self-control. *Journal of the Experimental Analysis of Behavior, 17*(1), 15–22.

Rachlin, H., Kagel, J. H., & Battalio, R. C. (1980). Substitutability in time allocation. *Psychological Review, 87*, 355–374.

Rasmussen, E. B., Reilly, W., Buckley, J., & Boomhower, S. R. (2012). Rimonabant reduces the essential value of food in the genetically obese Zucker rat: An exponential demand analysis. *Physiology & Behavior, 105*, 734–741.

Sanabria, F., Thrailkill, E. A., & Killeen, P. R. (2009). Timing with opportunity cost: Concurrent schedules of reinforcement improve peak timing. *Learning & Behavior, 37*(3), 217–229.

Segal, E. F. (1972). *Induction and the provenance of operants.* New York, NY: Academic Press.

Schindler, C. W., Panlilio, L. V., & Goldberg, S. R. (2002). Second-order schedules of drug self-administration in animals. *Psychopharmacology, 163*, 327–344.

Shull, R. L., & Pliskoff S. S. (1967). Changeover delay and concurrent schedules: Some effects on relative performance measures. *Journal of the Experimental Analysis of Behavior, 10*(6), 517–527.

Skinner, B. F. (1948). " Superstition" in the pigeon. *Journal of Experimental Psychology, 38*(2), 168–172.

Smethells, J. R., & Reilly, M. P. (2015). Intertrial interval duration and impulsive choice. *Journal of the Experimental Analysis of Behavior, 103*(1), 153–165.

Staddon, J. E. R., & Simmelhag, V. L. (1971). The "superstition" experiment: A reexamination of its implications for the principles of adaptive behavior. *Psychological Review, 78*(1), 3–43.

Stubbs, D. A., & Pliskoff, S. S. (1969). Concurrent responding with fixed relative rate of reinforcement. *Journal of the Experimental Analysis of Behavior, 12*(6), 887–895.

Williams, D. C., Saunders, K. J., & Perone, M. (2011). Extended pausing by humans on multiple fixed-ratio schedules with varied reinforcer magnitude and response requirements. *Journal of the Experimental Analysis of Behavior, 95*(2), 203–220.

van den Bos, W., & McClure S. M. (2013). Towards a general model of temporal discounting. *Journal of the Experimental Analysis of Behavior, 99*(1), 58–73.

Wearden, J. H. & Burgess, I. S. (1982). Matching since Baum (1979). *Journal of the Experimental Analysis of Behavior, 33*, 339–348.

Weller, R. E., Cook, E. W., Avsar, K. B., & Cox, J. E. (2008). Obese women show greater delay discounting than healthy-weight women. *Appetite, 51*(3), 563–569.

Williams, B. A. (1994). Conditioned reinforcement: Experimental and theoretical issues. *The Behavior Analyst, 17*(2), 261–285.

Yoon, J. H., Higgins, S. T., Heil, S. H., Sugarbaker, R. J., Thomas, C. S., & Badger, G. J. (2007). Delay discounting predicts postpartum relapse to cigarette smoking among pregnant women. *Experimental and Clinical Psychopharmacology, 15*(2), 176–186.

Image Credits

Fig 6.1: Federico Sanabria, from "Operant Conditioning," Encyclopedia of Animal Cognition and Behavior, ed. Jennifer Vonk and Todd K. Shackelford, p. 14. Springer Publishing Company, 2017.

Fig 6.2: Federico Sanabria, from "Operant Conditioning," Encyclopedia of Animal Cognition and Behavior, ed. Jennifer Vonk and Todd K. Shackelford, p. 15. Springer Publishing Company, 2017.

Fig 6.5: Adapted from Luís Oliveira, Leonard Green, and Joel Myerson, "Pigeons' Delay Discounting Functions Established Using a Concurrent-Chains Procedure," Journal of the Experimental Analysis of Behavior, vol. 102, no. 2. John Wiley & Sons, Inc., 2014.

Fig 6.7: Adapted from Timothy F. Elsmore, et al., "Reduction of Heroin Intake in Baboons by an Economic Constraint," Pharmacology Biochemistry and Behavior, vol. 13, no. 5. Elsevier B.V., 1980.

Fig 6.8: Adapted from Chesley J. Christensen, et al., "Essential Value of Cocaine and Food in Rats: Tests of the Exponential Model of Demand," Psychopharmacology, vol. 198, no. 2. Springer Verlag Heidelberg, 2008.

CPSIA information can be obtained
at www.ICGtesting.com
Printed in the USA
LVHW022118230821
695919LV00006B/44